Dave Craddock

Where They Burnt The Town Hall Down

Luton, the First World War and
the Peace Day Riots of 1919

Colophon

Author: ©Dave Craddock 1999.

First published July 1999

by The Book Castle.

2nd Edition published 2019

by Cultural Histories CIC.

Printed by Bartham Group Ltd, Luton.

Design by Noel Douglas [noeldouglas.net].

Assisted by Khatllen Cazacu and Nicole Cazacu

in the Guildford Street Press Studio at the

School of Art+Design, University of Bedfordshire.

Set in typefaces of the era.

Bureau Grotesque, Caslon, Futura, Latin CG and Robur.

All rights reserved

ISBN 978-1-5272-4296-8

Contents

Acknowledgments from David Craddock

I would like to give special thanks to the following people for their help and assistance in the preparation of this book. Elizabeth Adey, Keeper of Local History, Luton Museum Service, for her advice on the manuscript but mainly for her patience in response to my many pleas for help in locating research material.

Stephen Bunker, University of Luton, for reading the manuscript and for offering suggestions that greatly improved it. Tom Madigan for his kind help in checking details of the Luton Borough Police Force with me and for providing additional details on Chief Constable Charles Griffin. John Lally for giving me access to his thesis on the Luton War Tribunals together with Chris Turner and Bernard Dillon for making available their respective research on the 'New' Town Hall and Frank Chapman Scargill.

Thanks must also go to the following. Stuart Smith for his advice, support and continual cajoling. Darren Miles for details about his Grandfather, Henry William Miles and Dave Litchfield for the loan of postcards. Also to Gill and Roy Shepherd who served as readers and offered useful suggestions. (It was a pity the dessert went the same way as the Town Hall!)

I must also mention George Arthur Bacon whom I interviewed during the course of my research. In his nineties and still blessed with all of his faculties and a humorous personality, George, aged eighteen, was outside the Town Hall on the nights of 19th and 20th July. He managed to convey much of the violence of the riot but, when I asked, denied taking any part. Mind you, he told me, he didn't dare tell his father that he was even there. His father was Detective Sergeant Arthur Bacon of the Luton Borough Police.

I am indebted to Luton Museum Service, John Buckledee, Editor of the Luton News and Luton Central Library for permission to use photographs from their collections. Special mention must go to Chris Grabham, Rob Evans and Mark Stubbs. Where copyright is known I have acknowledged it. A thank you also to my son Owen for his encouragement and for keeping me amused when I was flagging.

Lastly, all my love to my wife, Val. Thank you for the encouragement, patience and for putting up with all the hours I spent married to the PC.

Dedicated to the memory of my grandfathers, L/Corporal Percy Craddock, Bedfordshire Regiment Sapper Arthur Wilfred Clark, East Anglian Division Royal Engineers who both fought in the Great War and my late father Joseph Craddock.

Acknowledgments from Mike McMahon and Steve Goodman

Cultural Histories CIC are very pleased to be publishing a second edition of Dave Craddock's wonderful book telling the story of the Luton Peace Day riots in 1919.

We are publishing the book to mark the centenary of the riots and because of the renewed interest shown in Luton and nationally about the riots and the part they played in the Town's history. We are very grateful to the Heritage Lottery Fund, the Luton and Bedfordshire Community Trust as part of the London Luton Airport Ltd Community Fund and the Arts Council England for supporting this book and many other projects marking the centenary year.

In particular we are very grateful to students and staff of the University of Bedfordshire arts and design department for improving the lay out and to Luton Culture and the Luton News for giving us permission to use the photographs and drawings.

The Cultural History CIC
Promoting Heritage for People and Places

Supported using public funding by
ARTS COUNCIL ENGLAND

heritage lottery fund
LOTTERY FUNDED

London Luton Airport Ltd
A Luton Council company

Bedfordshire and Luton Community Foundation

University of Bedfordshire

SCHOOL OF ART + DESIGN

GUILDFORD STREET PRESS

Where They Burnt The Town Hall Down

"We're a jolly lot of fellows, yes we are,
We're a jolly lot of fellows, yes we are,
For we come from Luton Town Where they
burnt the Town Hall down,
We're a jolly lot of fellows, yes we are."

Lyric to a song that groups of Lutonians were heard to sing
while on holiday in the late summer of 1919.

Where They Burnt The Town Hall Down

Foreward

In 1978 Dr John Dony, one of Luton's most respected historians, called the burning of the Town Hall 'the most outstanding event in the history of Luton in the last hundred years'. Yet for nearly eighty years the events of July 1919, which subsequently led to the trial of twenty-eight people at Bedford Assizes, have been almost totally neglected.

Only eight years after the riot William Austin, author of a two volume history of Luton, devoted a paltry nine line paragraph to the event which he described as an *'unfortunate incident'*. Since then other accounts, published and unpublished, have only touched the surface of the riot and are all subject to misinterpretation of the events which took place. The most comprehensive account so far has been a twenty-four page essay by John Dony published in 1978 by the Bedfordshire Historical Society. Even this is subject to inaccuracies.

Until now no full account of the Peace Day Riots has ever been published. Therefore I hope this book will provide readers with a much better understanding of the events that occurred during the summer of 1919.

The core of the book chronicles the events, including those that took place during the Great War, that led up to the Peace Day riots. A chapter on the old Town Hall, and its place in Luton's history is included, as it was the focal point of the riots. Details, now publicly available, of the subsequent trials at Luton Borough Court and Bedford Assizes are included for the first time, as is information on the rioters themselves.

As far as I am aware I have consulted all the available accounts, contemporary newspaper reports and witness statements. I have spoken to or received letters from a very small number of people who were outside the Town Hall on Peace Day. With one exception they were young children whose recollections mainly concern the procession and afternoon incidents. It does not matter for it is well known that over the years Lutonians were keen to forget that the riot ever took place and oral evidence, though often useful, has in this case I believe become distorted with the passage of time. In any event the wealth of detail available from the trials makes up for this deficiency.

The year of 1919 was one of great social and economic unrest in Britain. Serious industrial strikes in the mines, docks, railways and engineering, which even spread to the Police Federation, accounted for thirty-five million working days being lost during the year. Prices rose sharply, not least of all in housing rents and there was an extreme shortage 7 of property owing to suspended construction during the war. The unrest was so great that it was hardly surprising 1919 was called the year of the Labour offensive.

It was a year that also began with over three million men waiting to be demobilised from the armed forces. They were met with two major obstacles. The first was a poorly conceived and badly executed demobilisation programme. The second was that once processed ex-servicemen found that no provision had been made by the Government to help them obtain employment. They quickly became disillusioned.

For the first time however, demobbed men were not prepared to take things lying down and in the ex-servicemen's organisations, established during the war years, they had a voice through which their grievances could be aired.

It was units of the army that caused the first rumblings of unrest in January and February 1919. Armed soldiers marched from their camps into a number of towns and staged protests. Their demands, mainly for leave, were met quickly by the Government War Office.

In May and June the first significant trouble broke out. Race riots occurred in several seaports including Liverpool, Cardiff, Tyneside and Glasgow. They were directed mainly at West Indian seamen who had been recruited into the Merchant Navy during the war. Three people died in Cardiff and another in Liverpool.

There was an undercurrent of violence in London during July and August resulting in the 'battle of Wood Green' when hundreds of youths fought with the police. Serious rioting occurred in August in Liverpool when the police force went on strike resulting in hundreds of shops being looted. The army, called in to control the crowds, were forced to open fire killing one man and wounding another and making a total of three hundred and seventy arrests.

It was a series of disturbances that were centred around the official Peace Day celebrations however that involved demobbed soldiers. Saturday 19th July 1919 had been designated as national Peace Day and celebrations took place in towns and villages throughout the country. Unfortunately, disorder and violence broke out in Coventry, Wolverhampton, Swindon, Epsom and Salisbury.

But this is the story of what happened in Luton where the most serious trouble occurred and Lutonians woke up on a Sunday morning to find their Town Hall a gutted, smoke-charred ruin.

Dave Craddock November 1998

The Town Hall

Luton in the middle of the 19th century was on the eve of the expansion that would take it from a small market town to one of the largest industrial centres in the South of England. The 1851 Census gave the population as ten thousand six hundred and forty-eight. The township based along George Street, Park Street and Church Street was beginning to grow, predominantly in the districts of High Town and New Town. Unfortunately with the dense building programmes came large tracts of slum housing that inevitably led to an increase in crime and violence.

The establishment of the Luton County Court in 1846 was therefore considered a much-needed and very welcome addition to the town's growing needs. Held once a month and presided over by a circuit judge, the Court supplemented the Petty Sessions which had been held weekly in Luton since 1828 dealing in the main with cases of assault, poaching and vagrancy. The George Hotel housed the Sessions every Monday and initially the County Court sittings were held there also. One of the conditions of a local court being set up however was that the town undertook to provide a public building in which the proceedings could take place.

In the absence at this time of any local authority in the town (the Vestry, the chief ratepayers, together with a Board of Guardians answerable to the Quarter Sessions held at Bedford presided over the town's affairs) a number of eminent local businessmen among whom were Robert How, John Higgins and Richard Haselgrove, straw hat manufacturers, and Charles Austin a solicitor, got together to form a small company for the purpose of raising capital for the construction of a public building.

Calling themselves the Luton Town Hall Company, they offered shares for sale at a cost of £10 each. The Company acquired a prominent site at the western end of George Street at the junction of the roads for Bedford and Dunstable. Known as Cross Hill, a farm and stables had occupied the site, in the early part of the century, in front of which had stood a very imposing chestnut tree. But 1844 however the site was listed as 'three houses and garden owner Thomas Cook' in the Who's Who in the Town of Luton compiled by John Waller and based on the Tithe map of 1842 surveyed by John Cumberland.

The construction of the Town Hall was undertaken by a well-known local family firm, John Williams and Sons. Williams lived as did other of Luton's prominent citizens in George Street and he was responsible for building a large number of their properties and in 1836, the Union workhouse. He had three sons who had all trained as architects, as had Williams himself, and it was one of them Evan Owen Williams who was responsible for the design of the building which followed the classic style of architecture so popular in early Victorian years.

The Town Hall was opened on 27th August 1847 at a cost of £2,200, which did not include the purchase price of the land.

The external dimensions of the building measured approximately sixty feet in width, eighty feet in height and one hundred feet in depth. Steps from George Street led up to the main entrance and large double doors which opened into a vestibule. The vestibule led to five rooms of varying size on the ground floor and there were stairs down to a large cellar. A broad staircase led from the vestibule to the first floor which contained one large assembly room. Three casements opened out onto a small balcony from which the front of the building's upper façade consisted of four Tuscan Doric columns supporting a frieze and pediment along with three other pediments over the casements.

The largest ground floor room at the rear of the building was used by the County Court and Petty Sessions while the other rooms were rented out to various organisations within the town including the Luton Literary and Scientific Institution, the Savings Bank, the Great Northern Railway Ticket Office (and from 1870 the School Board). The assembly room was used for public meetings and entertainment.

Retail premises were built either side of the Town Hall and a warehouse in Dunstable Lane (now Upper George Street) was also built for William Higgins, a straw hat manufacturer. The two shops originally

Part of the tithe map of Luton surveyed by John Cumberland and published in 1842. To accompany it John Waller produced his Who's who in Luton'. Item number 354 listed as 'three houses and garden' is the site acquired by the Town Hall Company for its new building in 1846. Previously a farm, Cross Hill, had stood here.

Source: Luton Museum Service

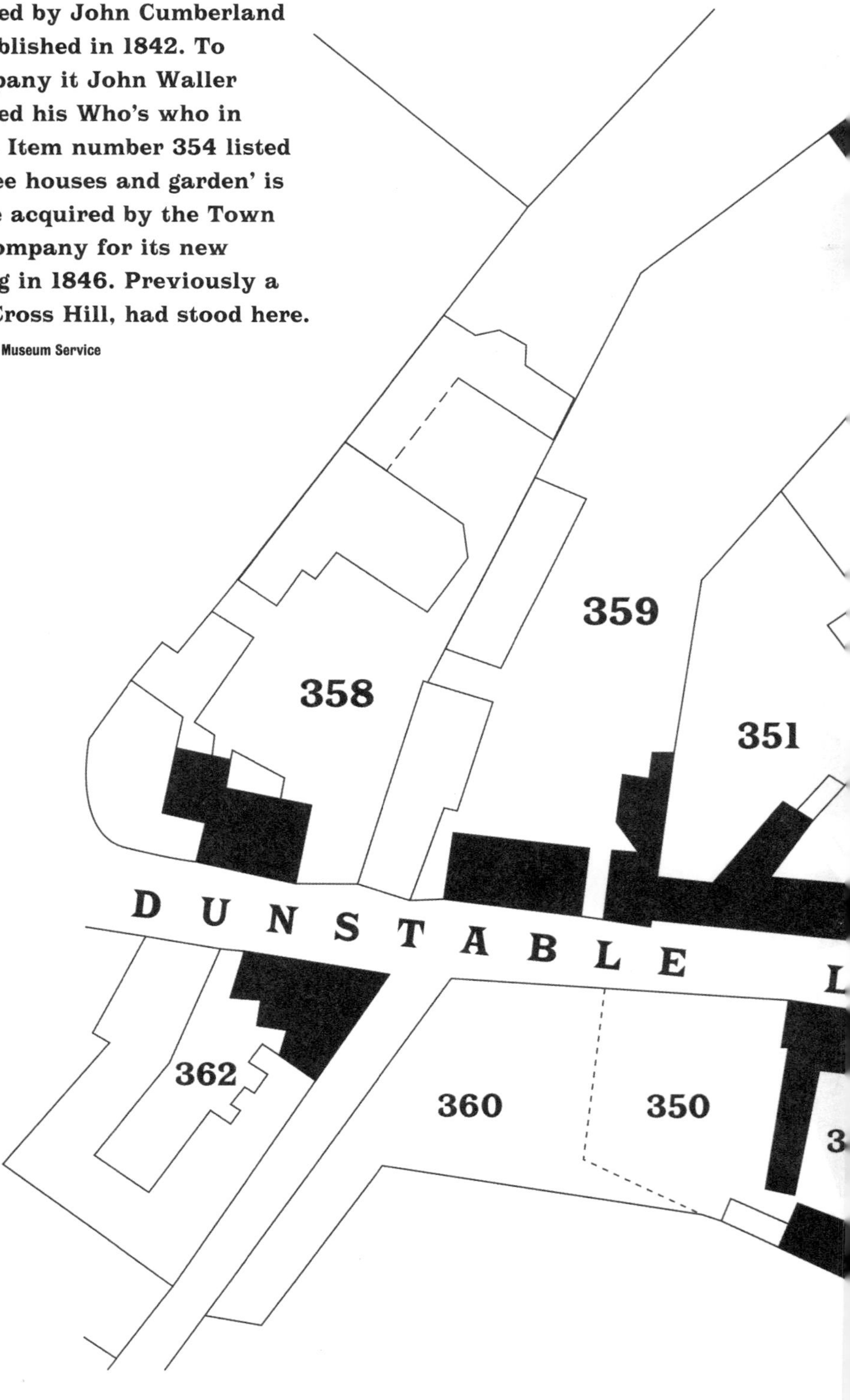

Where They Burnt The Town Hall Down

359

358

351

362

D U N S T A B L E L

360

350

3

traded as *F&M S Crawley*, a butcher, and *J. A. Taylor*, a fishmonger, whose tenure was very short as the premises were acquired by the local brewer, Thomas Sworder, who converted them into a public house, The Belgium Arms.

The Town Hall became the focal point for the community. On the 8th March 1852 it was the venue for an important meeting of local straw hat manufacturers, dealers and merchants at which they unanimously resolved to form a society which they called the Straw Hat Manufacturers Association. It was established to combat the dishonest practice of short measure in the plait coils which was prevalent in the industry. The Association was to last nearly thirty years through the heyday of the straw hat industry.

The 21st November 1854 saw a large crowd, mainly of women, gather outside the Town Hall. On a wet night they were there to attend a meeting concerning the bonnet trade. It soon became apparent no meeting was going to take place, which caused immense irritation to those who had waited in the foul weather. Various grievances were aired and feelings ran high eventually spilling over into disturbances in the town centre with damage being caused to a number of properties. Police reinforcements were requested and a number of people arrested.

(The Town Hall Luton)

Lithograph of the Town Hall by its architect Evan Owen Williams published in 1847. This is the earliest illustration of the building. The Williams family would be associated with the Town Hall throughout its history. Evan's father John built it and his son Herbert was a member of the Town Council that watched the Peace Day procession.
Source: Luton Central Library

In the latter part of 1856 a clock was installed in the pediment of the Town Hall to commemorate peace following the end of the Crimean war. Funding for the clock was met by public subscription. A small tower was also added to accommodate a single bell which struck on the hour. The Luton Times newspaper of 31st May 1856 reported the event as follows:

'On Thursday evening last a Soirée was held at the Town Hall, Luton, to celebrate the return of peace. The audience was one of the largest and most respectable that ever assembled in the Hall at a public concert ... and that it was intended to give the town of Luton, in commemoration of the peace of 1856, a standing memorial of the gratitude of the people for the return of peace, in the shape of a clock at the Town Hall. Since this project had been entertained upwards of £80 had been received for that object.'

The County Court continued to use the Town Hall until 1858 when the sittings were transferred to the newly-built Court house in Stuart Street. For the next twenty-five years the Town Hall was fully utilised by various organisations and societies in the town but it was never used for any purpose by the directors of the Town Hall Company. For them the venture was never the financial or commercial success they had obviously hoped for. A dividend was never paid to the shareholders and by 1873 the company was experiencing cashflow problems.

A special meeting of the company directors was called on 18th

Town Hall. Luton. Beds.

A stylised (lithograph of the Town Hall published in 1862. The clock and bell tower were added in 1856 to commemorate peace after the Crimean War. The clock was paid for by public subscription. When the building was put up for sale by the Town Hall Company the clock was the only item that was not part of the contents.
Source: Luton Museum Service

August of that year at which a motion to sell the Town Hall and dissolve the company was unanimously carried. The shareholders were called to an extraordinary general meeting on 2nd September at which the decision of the company directors were ratified by a vote of twenty to two. The shareholders also insisted on an amendment which stated that the building would not be sold for less than £2,000 without their approval.

The company directors held two further meetings. The first of the 14th October approved a deputation to meet the local Board of Health to advise them that they were putting the Town Hall up for sale and to ascertain whether or not the Board were interested in having first refusal. The second meeting held on the 28th October set the selling price of the Town Hall at £2,500. However, to enable the public to continue to use the building the directors were prepared to offer it to the Board of Health for £2,250.

The Luton Board of Health had been established on 19th June 1850 and acted with nearly all the powers that were then available to a Town Council, being responsible, among other things, for public order, highways, lighting and the care of its poor. The Public Health Act of 1848 instituted a Central Board of Health which had the authority to create local boards if petitioned by ten percent of its inhabitants. Following epidemics of cholera, typhoid and smallpox that had swept through the town resulting from a combination of fouled water supply, inadequate sewerage and almost non-existent refuge disposal, such a petition had been raised in Luton although not without some opposition. Over nearly twenty-five years the record of the Board of Health was quite impressive. Among its achievements were the introduction of an effective sewerage disposal system, the building of the Corn Exchange in 1869 replacing the dilapidated old market hall on Market Hill and in the same year the opening of the Plait Halls in Cheapside and Waller Street erected to house the straw plait market previously held in the open. They were also responsible for the first public baths in Waller Street opened in 1872.

The Board of Health met to consider the offer from the directors. Ironically the meeting was held at their usual place, the Town Hall. The chairman of the board was Frank Chapman Scargill, a prominent solicitor in the town and Clerk to the Justices. (He was at this time in the process of having a house and estate built at Bramingham Shott. Previously a farm, it was later to become Wardown Park.) The clerk to the board was George Bailey. Following the passing of a resolution the clerk was asked to *write to the Secretary of the Town Hall Company and inform him that this Local Board do not accept the offer of the Trustees of the Luton Town Hall Company for the sale of the Town Hall to this board for the sum of £2,250.'*

The Town Hall Company Directors met again on the 11th November at which the Board of Health letter rejecting their offer was read after which a resolution was passed to offer the building for general sale. Subsequently the following advertisement was placed in the town's two local newspapers, the Luton Times and the Luton Advertiser:

Luton Town Hall Company
The Directors of the above Company are prepared to sell by
private contract all the valuable property known as the Luton
Town Hall. For particulars apply to the Secretary, Instructions
to Secretary. Price £2,500. Fixtures at valuation.
Clock to be reserved for special arrangement with the Board
of Health.

Nothing happened for almost seven months and then on 10th June 1874 the Board of Health met and elected a committee to meet the Town Hall directors. Comprising Messrs. Cumberland, Lockhart and Chambers the object of the meeting was to *'ascertain whether they will accept the sum of £2,000 for the Town Hall, such an offer to be conditional upon the Local Government Board sanctioning the proposed purchase'.*

On 25th June the two sides met and the new offer was put forward. After a short adjournment the directors respectfully declined the revised offer but reiterated that they were still prepared to sell to the board at the original price of £2,250. The Board of Health met yet again on 30th June and passed another resolution to the effect that *'the clerk of this Board do write to the Secretary of the Town Hall Company and inform him that the Board will give the sum of £2,125 for the Town Hall'.*

A special meeting of the Company Directors was convened on the 9th July at which the following letter was read:

Luton Local Board of Health
July 1st 1874

Dear Sir,
I am directed by the Luton Local Board of Health to acknowledge
the receipt of your letter of the 26th ult. wherein you state that
the Directors of the Town Hall Company decline to sell the Town
Hall for £2,000.v
The Local Board having fully considered the whole matter, have
desired me to say that they will give the sum of £2,125 for the
Town Hall and no more, this offer to be final and subject to the
approval of the Local Government Board.

I am, Dear Sir
Yours Truly,
George Bailey, Clerk

After consideration of the letter it was moved that the Company Secretary write to the Board of Health to state that their final offer for the Town Hall was unanimously accepted.

Quite why the Board of Health reopened negotiations is not clear although William Austin in his History of Luton alludes to the fact that *'except for the public spirit of Mr George C. G. Lockhart and Mr John Higgins it (the Town Hall) would have passed into private hands'.*

Possibly interest from a private source prompted these two gentlemen, Lockhart a member of the Board and Higgins a Town Hall Company Director (and also a Board member) into being the prime movers in ensuring an agreement was reached between the two parties to prevent the building being lost to the townspeople of Luton.

The sale of the Town Hall was finally completed on 23rd March 1875. The Luton Town Hall Company went into voluntary liquidation and on 15th September 1875 the Company was finally wound up.

The manner in which the Board of Health had carried out their part in the purchase of the Town Hall helped to fuel the fire of those citizens who, for some time, had felt the town should petition for municipal borough status (among whom were some members of the Board). In 1860 two attempts at establishing the town as a separate borough had failed. With the town growing rapidly many felt there was now a need for a more efficient and democratic form of local government. A request to call a public meeting was put before the churchwardens and overseers. Luton was still a parish and they were the only body who could give approval to such a request. At 3.00pm on 10th December 1874 a large audience assembled at the Plait Hall in Cheapside. The chairman of the meeting was Evan Owen Williams and its purpose to *'consider the desirability of applying for a Charter of Incorporation for Luton and to take such steps as may be found necessary in relation to the same'.*

A large majority were in favour of applying for the Charter although there was a body of objectors led by Frank Chapman Scargill, the Board of Health chairman. One of their arguments was that while Lutonians were industrious and worthy they were not so amenable to control as those persons who lived at Bedford! The for lobby had their way and on 26th February 1876 amid much excitement the town received its Charter of Incorporation. Within the charter were details of the boundaries for the new North, East and West wards and the number of Councillors that were to serve on them.

Luton's first Municipal election took place of 18th May 1876 when thirty-seven candidates contested the three new wards with six members being returned for each ward. Evan Owen Williams' name was again prominent as he had been appointed the returning officer. Among the newly elected councillors were a number of the now defunct Board of Health members including George Lockhart.

The first meeting of the Town Council took place in the Town Hall on the 26th May. The granting of the Charter had put the responsibility for the building into the hands of the Corporation and it now became the home to the new local authorities. At the meeting, William Bigg, who had led the campaign for borough status, was unanimously elected to serve as Luton's first mayor. At a further meeting held on 10th June George Bailey, clerk to the former Board of Health, was appointed to the position of Town Clerk.

In 1882 the Luton Literary and Scientific Institution was dissolved and so ended its tenancy at the Town Hall which had lasted almost thirty-five years. The Institution's library which had been housed in the Town Hall was presented to the new Free Library which opened on the 9th February 1883.

Throughout the town's 19th century expansion, local and national politics had leaned heavily in favour of the Liberal Party and their commitment to Free trade. National politics had come to the town in 1884 when all male householders received the right to vote and the Luton or South Bedfordshire constituency was created. It was no surprise therefore that in the general election of 1885 the Liberal candidate Cyril Flower was elected with a majority of two thousand, two hundred and nine. A large crowd gathered in the town centre to hear the returning officer read the result from the Town Hall balcony, a scene that would be repeated on many occasions. A very popular Member of Parliament, Flower held the seat in 1886 and 1891 before being created Baron of Battersea and Overstrand and moving to the House of Lords. The by-election that followed was won by the Liberals but their candidate Howard Whitbread (a member of the brewing family) proved unpopular with his party and for the general election of 1895 he was replaced by a Macclesfield businessman, Thomas Gair Ashton. Many people in the town expected the contest between Ashton and his opponent Lieutenant Colonel Oliver Thomas Duke, standing as a Liberal Unionist, to be close and so it turned out with Ashton winning the seat by a slim majority of one hundred and eighty-six votes. The declaration of the result at the Town Hall on 24th July however was the signal for rioting to break out in the town centre.

The riot had as its cause the decision, by the town's most prominent solicitor at the time Mr H. W. Lathom, to switch his allegiance from Duke to Ashton midway through the campaign, a move that was considered by many Unionists to have significantly affected the result. The windows of Lathom's office in King Street were smashed together with many others in the town. Assistance was obtained from the Metropolitan police and a large force of officers arrived in the town around 1.00am and the streets were quickly cleared. The following night there was a further minor outbreak of stone throwing. A number of people appeared at the magistrates' court but the majority of the cases were dismissed without convictions.

The early years of the Council saw an increase in the number of Corporation departments and the need arose to provide additional office space to accommodate them. In 1887, Queen Victoria's Jubilee year, the Council put into motion a scheme to acquire the properties adjoining the Town Hall. Discussions had also taken place within Council meetings with regard to the provision of new Municipal buildings and it was agreed the acquisition of adjacent properties would give the Council a bigger site should they wish to develop it. The initial purchase was The Belgium Arms public house from brewers Roberts and Wilson in 1887 which was turned into offices for the Sanitary Inspector, Tolls Collector and Inspector of Weights and Measures. This was followed in 1893 by Rossons' shop next to the Town Hall plus further retail premises andwarehouse in Manchester Street. The shop was utilised as the Food Office and other offices were created to house the Borough Accountant and Town Hall manager. In 1897 a butcher's shop and three cottages, Forsters Yard, also in Upper George Street completed the Council's purchases. By the turn of the century their acquisition policy had resulted in a somewhat miscellaneous collection of buildings which were connected by winding stairways and passages from which they conducted their affairs. The site however was ideally suited for future development.

The Town Hall c.1880. The Belgium Arms public house is on the left. One of Luton's most popular inns of the period, it was purchased by the Council in 1887 and incorporated into the Town Hall as part of their site expansion. Rosson's shop followed suit in 1893.
F. Thurston/Source: Luton Museum Service

Plan of the Town Hall c.1887. The plan shows the ground floor consisting of the vestibule, five rooms and the staircase leading to the assembly room. Fosters Yard was incorporated in 1899.

Source: Luton Museum Service

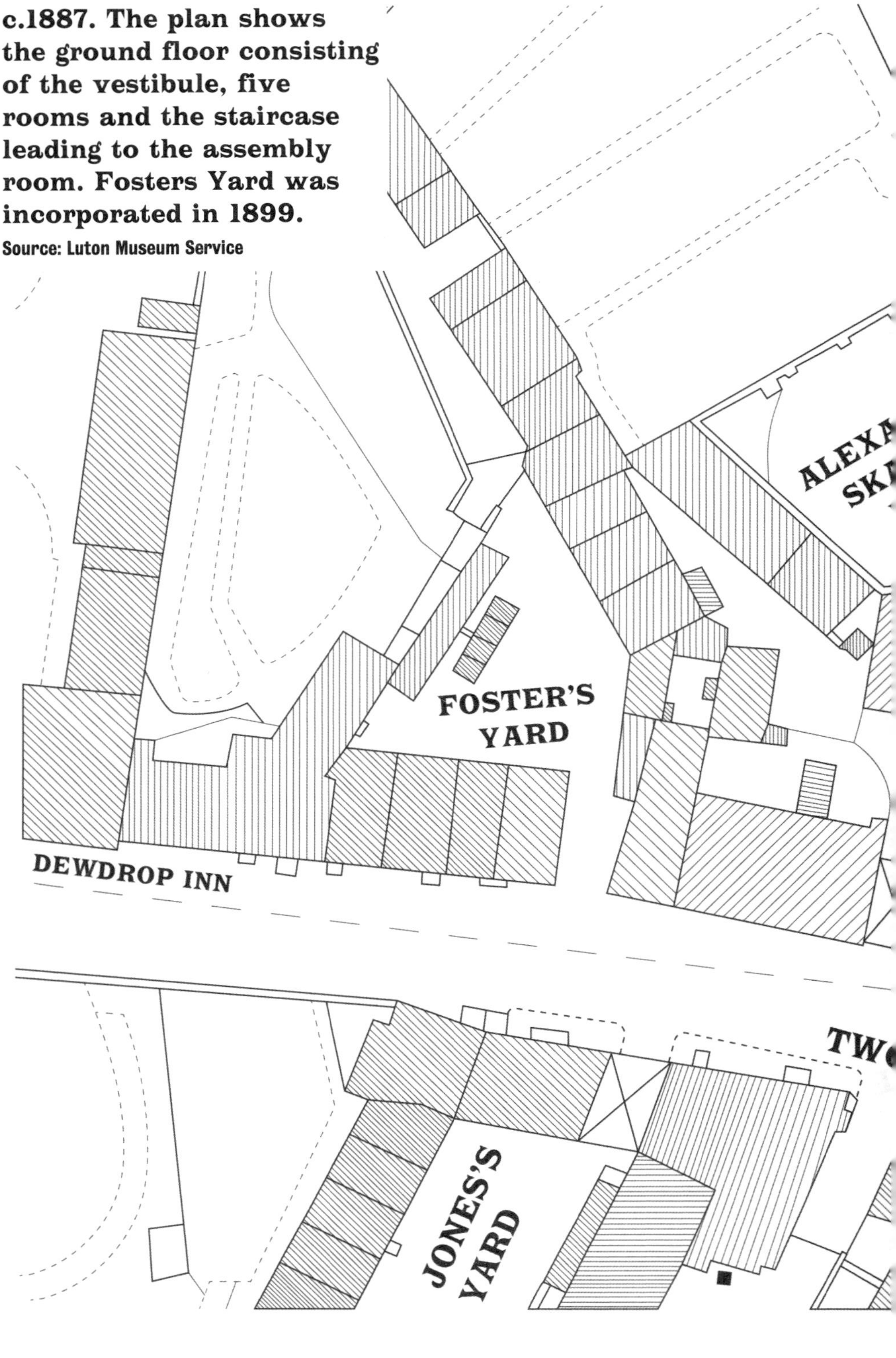

ALEXA
SK

FOSTER'S
YARD

DEWDROP INN

TW

JONES'S
YARD

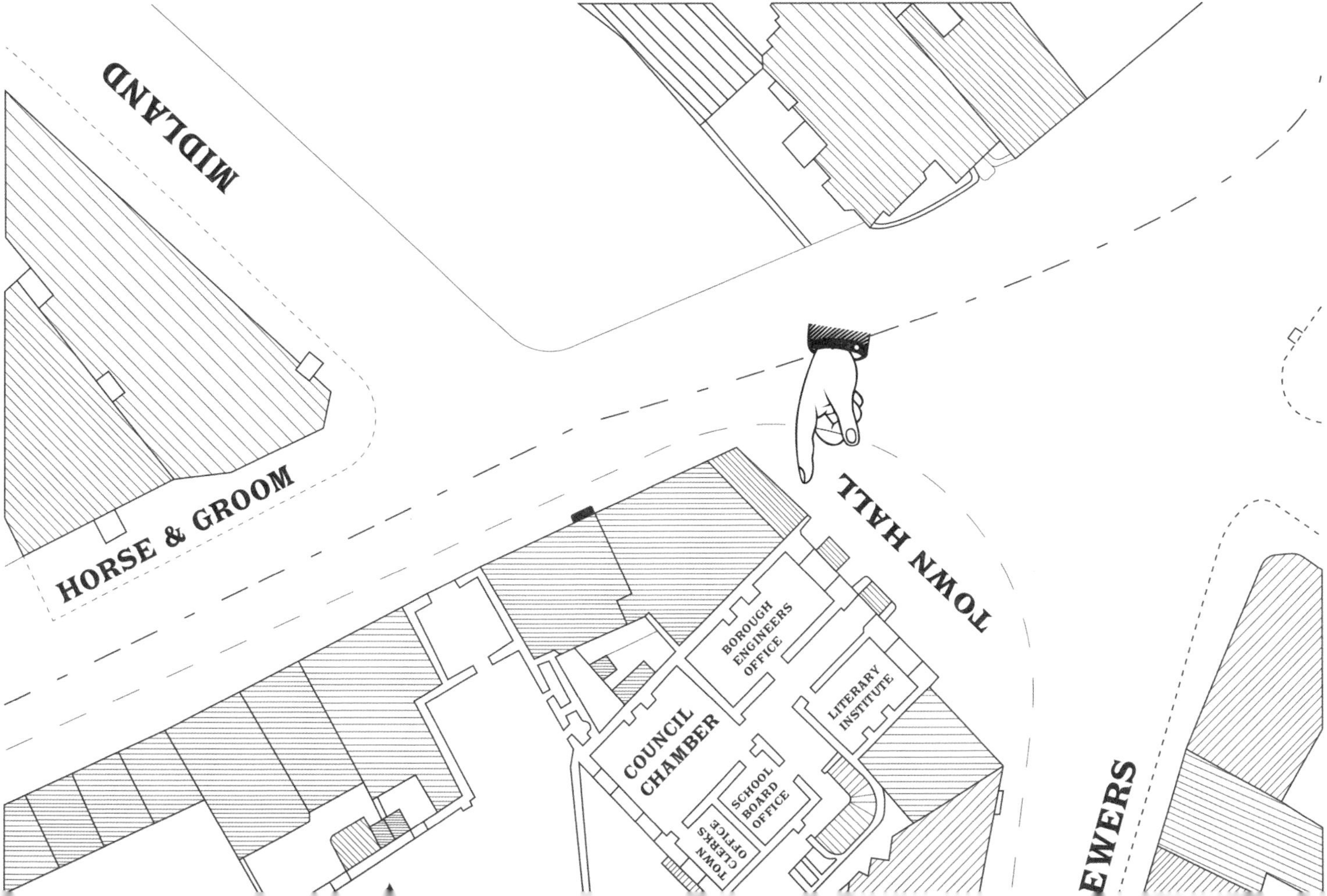

HORSE & GROOM

MIDLAND

COUNCIL CHAMBER

TOWN CLERKS OFFICE

SCHOOL BOARD OFFICE

BOROUGH ENGINEERS OFFICE

LITERARY INSTITUTE

TOWN HALL

EWERS

As the twentieth century dawned, concern grew at Council meetings over the town's almost total reliance on its hat industry. There was a growing realisation that any collapse in the trade could spell economic and social disaster. the Council, in a surprisingly far-sighted move, took the decision to attract new industry to the town and to achieve their goal pinned their faith in the future of electricity. The result was the building of the Corporation owned Electricity Works, opened by Lord Kelvin in July 1901, which made cheap power available in the town to both industrial and private sectors.

Allied to this, the New Industries Committee, composed of members of the Council and Chamber of Commerce, was established. Responsible for attracting new industry, the committee set out on a widespread advertising campaign that was rooted in the cheap price of the electricity, low rates and attractive land prices together with Luton's close proximity to London.

This foresight shown by the Council brought them unparalleled success and in the first decade of the century many firms were enticed to relocate to the town. Among them were a number that were to establish themselves as major employers in the years to come, Vauxhall Motors, Hayward Tyler, George Kent and the Skefco Ball Bearing Company. It also heralded a new industrial age and Luton would soon become a centre for the engineering assembly line.

The year of 1911 saw the Town Council petitioning a Bill in Parliament. Among items included within the Bill was the right to build a new Town Hall on the Corporation's existing site. A House of Commons Committee met on 14th March and questioned the Mayor, Alderman Albert Wilkinson, Town Clerk Bruce Penny and Borough Surveyor John Tomlinson on the proposals for a new building. No definite scheme had been drawn up at this stage but the Borough Surveyor had estimated a cost of £55,000 based on Municipal buildings in other towns and the building cost per cubic foot. On 18th August the 'Luton Corporation Act', as it was called was passed by Parliament. Part 111, Item 22 of the Act read as follows:

'The Corporation may with the consent of the Local Government
Board for the purposes of this section on lands already belonging
to them erect and construct and hold furnish equip maintain
insure and carry on a town hall municipal buildings police

station petty sessional court public hall assembly rooms and other public buildings with all necessary and suitable offices committee rooms entertainment rooms ante rooms refreshment rooms kitchens cloakrooms lavatories gardens outbuildings conveniences and appurtenances and may for the purpose thereof alter adapt extend or otherwise deal with existing buildings belonging to the Corporation and may provide erect and maintain shops and offices as part of any such building or buildings.'

The year of 1911 also saw another by-election in the town. Thomas Gair Ashton had proved an extremely popular MP and had held the seat for sixteen years. Like Cyril Flower before him he moved to the Lords as Lord Ashton of Hyde. The election saw another Liberal victory when their candidate, Cecil Harmsworth, easily won the seat. Previously MP for Droitwich, Harmsworth was the younger brother of the press barons Lords Northcliffe and Rothermere.

The following year, 1912, saw the resignation of Bruce Penny, the Town Clerk of Luton. Arguably the most important and influential member of the Corporation, the Town Clerk was the Chief Administrative Officer and his role was to oversee the various committees of the Council and to ensure that the town's affairs were run efficiently. All Council officers were answerable to the Town Clerk who also had overriding jurisdiction in all matters of law.

William Smith, Town Clerk of Luton 1912-1932. Born in Liverpool, Smith was the driving force behind the Corporation but his tactiturn and aloof demeanour made him unpopular with many Lutonians

F. Thurston/Source: Luton Museum Service

On 3rd September 1912, William Smith was appointed to succeed Penny as Town Clerk for Luton. Born in Liverpool on 4th January 1869, Smith had commenced his career as a clerk in Cardiff in 1890. Three years later he was appointed Assistant Town Clerk at Colchester where he also qualified as a solicitor and in May 1907 he took up the position of Town Clerk at Chelmsford. One of his most important assignments whilst at Chelmsford was to see through an extension to the Borough boundaries, part of which involved conducting proceedings before

Committees of both Houses of Parliament.

One of nearly seventy candidates who applied for the post, six were selected to be interviewed, with Smith being the only one who had already served in the position of Town Clerk.

At his interview he clearly impressed the Council selection panel with his apparent skills and trustworthiness and it soon became clear he was the outstanding candidate for the position. On his appointment it was remarked that Smith should prove a valuable asset to the public service of the town. He also took up the duties of solicitor for the Corporation.

A tall imposing man, invariably seen dressed in wig and gown, his demeanour was rather forbidding and stern which made him appear aloof from the public. He could also be highly strung and emotional. People who came to know him however regarded him as a man of great generosity who could display a good sense of humour. In his position as Town Clerk, Smith always displayed a dignified presence and was to fully justify his appointment but at the cost of becoming a very unpopular figure with many Lutonians.

Through late 1913 and into 1914 the Corporation were giving the practicalities of proceeding with a scheme for new Municipal buildings serious consideration. The men who now sat on the Council had shared in the success of the first decade. They were self-made men, businessmen and manufacturers, many still in the hat industry, and for the most part Liberals, maintaining the philosophy of their predecessors. Many served on the Chamber of Commerce and some were related by marriage. They had in effect become a clique, comfortable in the knowledge that they were unchallenged from other sectors of the community. Prosperity for the town had gone hand in hand with prosperity for these men but they also possessed a genuine affection for Luton and the need to make their town successful. They considered the time was now right to replace the ageing buildings of the Town Hall conplex. The coming of war caused plans to be shelved though as Councillors turned their attention to more urgent matters.

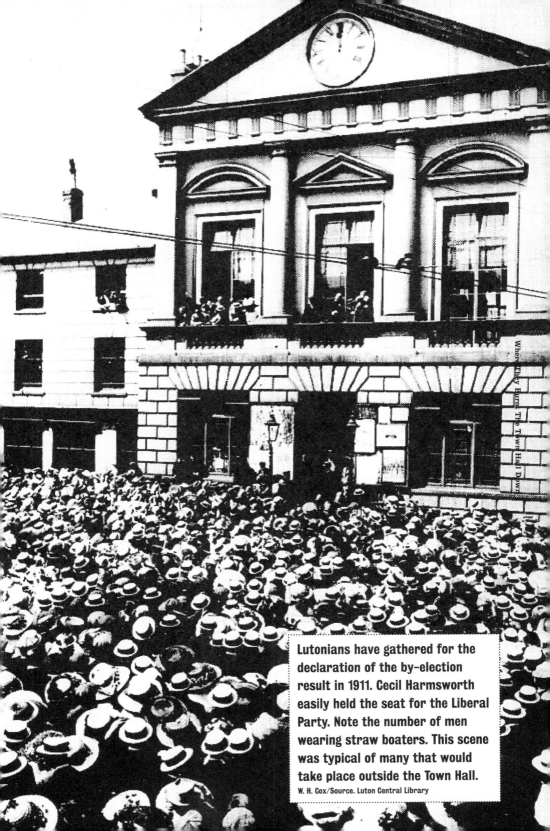

Lutonians have gathered for the declaration of the by-election result in 1911. Cecil Harmsworth easily held the seat for the Liberal Party. Note the number of men wearing straw boaters. This scene was typical of many that would take place outside the Town Hall.

W. H. Cox/Source. Luton Central Library

The Town Hall c.1915 in its final form with all the incorporated properties which have been rendered to match with the original building. The Council now had an excellent site for their new Municipal building proposed in the Luton Corporation Act of 1911.
Source: Luton Museum Service

Where They Burnt The Town Hall Down

The Home Front 1914-1918

O n 4th August 1914 Britain declared war on Germany after an ultimatum calling for them to withdraw from Belgium had been ignored. The regimental strength of the regular British army was two hundred and forty-four thousand, of whom eighty thousand were already on duty overseas. In support were the part time Territorial Army organised on a regional basis and of similar strength to the regular army. Their primary role was to act as a home defence force in the event of war. Few people saw them as front line troops including Lord Kitchener who had recently been appointed as Secretary of State for War. His belief was that the army strength should be increased through a volunteer system and to this end Parliament authorised an increase of five hundred thousand men on 6th August. The first recruiting posters appeared the following day calling for one hundred thousand men to sign on for a period of three years. The widely held belief that the war would be over within six months was not a view shared by Kitchener.

In Luton hundreds of men answered Kitchener's call to arms and were assimilated into the various regiments of the regular army while the part time Territorials were mobilised into their three local units, the largest of which was the 1st/5th Battalion of the Bedfordshire Regiment. They were one of a number of Territorial battalions who had volunteered for active service abroad in the event of war and a compromise had been reached with Lord Kitchener that these units could go, provided they were up to full battalion strength and had undergone a training period of at least six months. To this end the 5th Bedford's moved to Bury St. Edmunds, their appointed War Station, while back in Luton a committee was formed to oversee the task of recruitment.

Mass meetings were organised similar to that held on Thursday evening, 10th September 1914. Three thousand people assembled in Park Square to listen to rousing speeches given by Mayor W. Primett and the town's MP, Cecil Harmsworth. Representing the 5th Battalion was Luton born Major Edgar W. Brighten.

Harmsworth's speech was full of jingoistic rhetoric typical of rallying speeches given by political figures at a time when the overwhelming feeling in the country was that the war would be over quickly. Having, he said, served a term as a volunteer in peace time with nothing very exciting about it, how much more fortunate were the young men of today to be able to put on the King's khaki and enrol themselves at once among the defenders of their country. At the closure of the meeting everyone moved to the Corn Exchange where new recruits were cheered by the crowd as they climbed the steps to enlist.

On mobilisation, troops from the 2nd/1st North Midlands Division Territorial Battalion had been sent to Luton for their training and were being housed at temporary camps at Stockwood Park, Round Green and the Moor as well as being billeted with families. In late September they were reviewed twice in quick succession, firstly by King George and then two weeks later by Lord Kitchener. On both occasions the parade took place at Luton Hoo Park. On the death of Sir Julius Wernher in 1912, his wife, Alice had become Lady of the Manor of Luton. She had offered use of her estate to the War Office which had been readily accepted. A purpose-built hutted camp was later established at Biscot, on the north edge of the town, replacing the temporary camps.

By mid 1915 the 1st/5th Bedford's were ready for active service. Knowing that they could embark at any time the battalion took part in a sixty mile march around the county over a period of three days. Dressed in full service kit they left their camp at St. Albans, having moved there from Bury St. Edmunds, and made their way to Dunstable and then on to Bedford. Civic receptions were held for them in both towns. Throughout the three days the weather was very hot. On Saturday 2nd June they were due to march into Luton in the early afternoon but the battalion rested at Barton, four miles north of the town, to let the fierce heat of the day pass.

Now under the command of Edgar Brighten who had been promoted to the rank of Lieutenant Colonel in early 1915, the eight hundred strong battalion finally marched into Luton at precisely

The 1st l5th Territorial Battalion of the Bedfordshire Regiment outside the Town Hall 2nd June 1915. Town Councillors and other Civic dignitaries stand on the platform while the Regimental Band plays the National Anthem. Lieutenant Colonel Edgar Brighten, the Battalion's commanding officer, is on horseback facing the band. Source: Luton Central Library

7.00pm, manoeuvred in George Street and came to attention. In front of the Town Hall a temporary platform had been erected on which waited the civic dignitaries including members of the Corporation and the South Beds Recruiting Committee.

Mayor Primett welcomed the battalion on behalf of the town and gave a short speech. Lt. Col. Brighten replied thanking the Mayor for the reception and saying that the battalion felt that they had come home. He then called for three cheers from his men and the regimental band played the national anthem before they marched off to Luton Hoo where they bivouacked for the night and those men who lived in the town were allowed to go home for the Saturday night.

It was not until the battalion had marched out of the town centre that the vast size of the crowd that had watched the battalion became apparent. George Street thronged with people and older inhabitants considered it to be the largest gathering ever seen in the town centre. (It was a scene that was to be repeated four years later.) On Sunday morning the battalion attended church parade at Luton parish church of St. Marys and spent the rest of the day relaxing before setting off for St. Albans in the evening to return to their camp.

On the 26th July the battalion embarked for a destination

'somewhere out East' and on 11th August landed at Suvla Bay on the Gallipoli peninsula. As part of the 54th East Anglian division they went into action on the 15th August, immediately suffering heavy casualties, among whom was the brother of Lieutenant Colonel Brighten, killed late in the day's fighting. After the disaster of Gallipolli, the 5th Bedford's were to travel to Egypt and subsequently take part in the campaign in the Middle East.

By late 1915, a large drop in the number of volunteers, casualties and increasing demands for manpower in the munitions factories was leading to a crisis in the army. In October 1915 the 'Derby Scheme' was introduced. Named after its originator, the newly appointed director of recruiting, Lord Derby, the aim of the scheme was for men between the ages of eighteen and forty-one to attest their willingness to serve, if and when they were called upon to do so. Assurances were given to married men who attested that they would not be called up until all single men had joined.

Luton's initial contribution was a large recruitment rally held on the afternoon of Saturday 2nd October. A procession toured the town

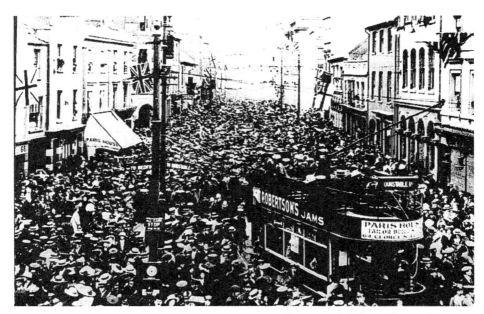

The scene in George Street after the departure of the 1st l5th Battalion to Luton Hoo. The crowd was considered to be the largest ever to have gathered in the town centre. Source: Luton Central Library

stopping at several points where speeches urged men to join up. The rally on this occasion was on behalf of the 3rd/5th Territorial battalion which had been established in May 1915 to supply drafts of men to its front line battalion. Included in the procession were the colours of the 5th battalion which were paraded in the town for the first time. Escort to the colour was provided by men of the 3rd/5th whose commanding officer Major R. E. B. Orelbar was also present. At the conclusion of the procession a rally was held outside the Town Hall presided over by Mayor Primett. Cecil Harmsworth and Lady Wernher were also present.

The *'Derby Scheme'* ran for three months. It was not a success. Just over three hundred thousand men had attested. Conscription was inevitable and came in January 1916 with the Military Service Act. All single men, not in reserved occupation, were to be called up and in May the Act was extended to include all married men. With conscription came the creation of the War Tribunal. This was a means whereby men could appeal against their enlistment. Thousands of local tribunals were established across the country to pass judgement on exemption in four areas — economic distress, essential war work, ill-health and conscientious objection. Guidelines suggested that the composition of these tribunals should be made up of impartial men with balanced judgement who were not necessarily from the local authorities. Not coming under any central government control the tribunals ultimately worked as much against the War Office as with it in being able to make their recommendations based on their own local economic needs.

The Luton War Tribunal Committee met this criteria well comprising as it did five Councillors, two employers and two men from the Labour movement together with a representative from the War Office. Town Clerk William Smith was appointed clerk to the tribunal. With his knowledge and experience of the legal system as solicitor for the Council, Smith invariably advised on points of law and acted in the role of cross examiner for the Tribunal, though he was not allowed a vote. In the two years that it was in session the Luton Tribunal members reached agreement on their decisions with few problems, but hostility did break out on occasions invariably involving the military representative. Arguments tended to be over men involved in the hat trade, which had been classed as a non-essential industry, but of which the tribunal members were naturally extremely protective. Smith also strongly defended the self employed, who were always in danger of ruin if conscripted, but it did not help his popularity with working class Lutonians

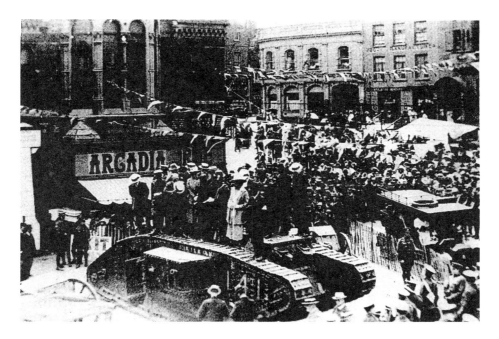

One of the numerous fund-raising events seen in Luton during the war. This was the 'Tank Bank' held in July 1918. This savings week was opened by Lady Wernher, standing on the tank to the right of the Mayor, Councillor Dillingham. The event attracted much interest from Lutonians, the majority of whom had never seen a tank, and nearly £500,000 was raised during the week. Source: Luton Central Library

For the first sixteen months of the war Wardown House had been occupied by the Military and used for housing troops who were training in the area and had fallen ill or suffered accidents. The mansion and estate built forty years earlier for Frank Chapman Scargill was now owned by the Town Council.

With the departure of the North Midlands Field Ambulance in November 1915 the Council offered use of the building, rent free, to the nurses of the local branch of the Volunteer Aid Detachment (VAD) of the Red Cross Society. Some modifications were carried out internally to accommodate sixty-two beds for wounded personnel and the VAD took possession at the end of January 1916. The house was to be fully utilised for the rest of the war.

Through 1916 money raising events became commonplace in the town. Funds were raised for the Red Cross, the YMCA and for the various relief funds set up both locally and nationally. These included the Prince of Wales fund and the Belgian Relief fund. A number of refugees had been living in the town since 1914 and had integrated well into the community.

The Luton War Pensions Committee was also established in April 1916, under the Naval and Military Pensions Act of November 1915, to administer the pensions of servicemen or their dependants in the town.

The board of Agriculture authorised local authorities to take possession of unoccupied and common land together with public parks for the purpose of growing food. It was the birth of the allotment system and in Luton came under the auspices of the Council Parks Committee. Potatoes grew in abundance in Wardown Park.

In September the town received the sad news that Alex Pigott Wernher, the nineteen year old son of Sir Julius and Lady Alice, had been killed. On the 11th September his regiment, the 1st Welsh Guards was in action at Ginchy in France. He had then been wounded in the leg and was being dragged back from no-man's land when he was shot dead.

December 1916 saw the end of Herbert Asquith as Prime Minister. Having entered the war as leader of the Liberal Party he had been forced to form a Coalition government in May 1915 after serious problems with the supply of munitions to the armed forces. His coalition comprised Liberals and Conservatives and, for the first time a member of the Labour Party, Arthur Henderson. Luton's MP, Cecil Harmsworth, had been appointed Under Home Secretary within the administration. Criticism of Asquith's leadership mounted after the disastrous Dardanelles campaign and stalemate on the Somme coupled with its horrendous casualties. On 7th December the fiery Welsh Liberal, David Lloyd George, a much more charismatic figure who had served on the Coalition as Minister of Munitions, was appointed Prime Minister.

As the war entered its fourth year the high hopes and excitement of an early victory had evaporated. Lord Kitchener had been right but he had lost his life along with all the crew aboard HMS Hampshire when it was struck by a mine and sunk in the Atlantic Ocean in June 1916. A general war weariness had begun to set in and with it came an increase in labour unrest which resulted in a series of unofficial strikes throughout the country in May 1917. The origins of the strike could be found in the Munitions of War Act 1915. The newly created Ministry of Munitions had brought in the Act under which the Trade Unions had given up the right to strike and had agreed to the suspension of restrictive practices. This ensured continuous production in factories with the introduction of semi, unskilled and female labour into what were previously skilled jobs, a dilution of labour. In return the government had agreed to maintain the skilled pay rate for all workers but primarily had given recognition to Labour and the Trade Unions as a partner in the war economy with Arthur Henderson being made a member of the Cabinet. In December 1916 the 'Trade Card Agreement' was introduced whereby the government allowed decisions over the exemption of skilled workers in munitions factories to be left in the hands of the union, the Amalgamated Society of Engineers.

In March 1917 the government announced that it proposed to extend the dilution of labour to private work and they followed this in April with the withdrawal of the Trade Card Scheme. Before any official government action however, an engineering company in Rochdale anticipated the extension of dilution which resulted in an immediate strike on 3rd May. With the Trade Union agreement for no strikes it was left to the local shop stewards to call the stoppage. It was the catalyst for national and local grievances to be aired throughout the country and resulted in two hundred thousand men walking out in the *May Munitions Strikes*.

In Luton around a thousand members of the Amalgamated Society of Engineers walked out on Friday evening, 11th May, refusing to return to work until the grievances were addressed. Word of the stoppage quickly spread which resulted in a demonstration by Military personnel, unhappy at the walkout, at the Luton Labour Club in Bute Street. Mayor John Staddon pacified the situation and prevented the Military from intervening in the dispute. On the Saturday morning strike leaders met Staddon and William Smith at the Town Hall and the two men were invited to address a mass meeting that was held in the afternoon at the Luton Town Football Ground. Again small demonstrations were held by members of the Military as well as civilians but there was no trouble. Staddon had some degree of sympathy for the strikers and asked them to conduct themselves in an honourable way and to stay within the law. Concern that there would be trouble on Saturday night was ill founded and the weekend passed without any incidents.

A further mass meeting was held behind closed doors at the football ground on the Tuesday at the end of which a vote was taken. Applause greeted the decision to remain on strike which was carried by a huge majority. Negotiations between the government and the Shop Stewards Committee held in London on the Tuesday evening broke down and with no sign of a breakthrough further mass meetings were held at the football ground each morning. On Friday evening came news that eight shop steward leaders had been arrested and charged under the powers of the 'Defence of the Realm Act' (D.O.R.A.) but this news coincided with the Ministry of Munitions agreeing to meet the A.S.E. Executive on the Saturday morning.

It was just after 6.00pm on Saturday when Luton received the news that the A.S.E. were recommending a return to work on the Monday morning and it was a cheerful and somewhat relieved group of men who gathered for the final time on the Sunday morning to accept their executive's decision.

The personal intervention of the Prime Minister had paved the way for the ending of the strike. He had agreed that the government would look at all complaints and negotiate with the Trade Union leaders in dealing with the problems. To this end a series of Commissions of Enquiry into industrial unrest were established in eight areas of the country. The contentious proposal for private dilution was dropped and the strike leaders were released and all charges dropped.

In Luton the strikers all returned to work on the Monday morning after ten days of stoppage. It was the first time that serious industrial unrest had come to the town. Mayor John Staddon had made daily appeals, on behalf of the Corporation, for the men to return to work but the national nature of the dispute had left him powerless to intervene. It was not to be long though before the Council were to encounter further industrial action and this time of a local nature that was to pose the biggest challenge to authority that a Luton Council had ever had to face.

Through the years of war, food prices had risen slowly and by 1917 shortages began to develop. The Ministry of Food had been established in 1916 and Lloyd George had appointed a Food Controller, Lord Devonport, to oversee the control of food supplies. In response to the shortages the Food Controller made an appeal for voluntary rationing on 3rd February 1917. It was totally unsuccessful. The shortages intensified and with them came the birth of the British tradition of the orderly queue. On 30th May 1917 Lord Devonport resigned and the

Ministry was taken over by Lord Rhondda. In August 1917 he issued a directive to all local authorities setting up Food Control Committees throughout the country.

With the shortages came profiteering. High profit margins of traders and shopkeepers came in for constant criticism from working class leaders and Labour politicians as well as a large section of the press. The profiteering caused much discontent nation-wide and in Luton dissatisfaction started to appear in October 1917.

The Luton Food Control Committee with John Staddon as its chairman comprised twelve members. There were seven Councillors, two representatives of the Luton Tradesman's Association, one from the Co-operative Society, Mrs Staddon who ostensibly represented the townswomen and a representative from the Luton Trades and Labour Council. Town Clerk William Smith acted as the Executive Officer.

The Luton Trades and Labour Council had been established in 1904 to represent the interests of eleven unions in the town. By 1917 its membership was around seven thousand. From the outset they requested three members to sit on the Food Committee claiming one was insufficient to represent their interests but various representations made to the Town Council were turned down.

On 11th October 1917 the Trades and Labour Council passed a resolution withdrawing their member, Mr P. J. Banks, in protest over the composition of the Food Control Committee. It was, they said, not representative of the working class majority and the Labour movement in general. The resolution was discussed by the full Council at its next meeting and a number of Councillors took a rather officious and sarcastic stance over the issue. The Trades and Labour Council were not in a position to withdraw their member they said, as he had been appointed to serve for a year. However if the gentleman concerned felt that he was not up to the job he was quite welcome to resign and the Council would consider another nomination. Subsequently Mr Banks offered his resignation. Over the next couple of months further problems began to mount for the Food Control Committee.

Cases of violation of the 'Meat Prices Order' came to the attention of the Trades Unions and were made public in the press. In short, some butchers in the town had been caught charging higher prices for meat than those set by the Food Controller. The Food Committee were brought to task for not doing their job and leaving the general public ill-informed of set prices. Worse was to follow. It became clear that a number of shopkeepers were making deliveries to private houses while working class women and children were queuing for hours for the same provisions. Criticism was also directed at the stores of 'Oakley Bros.'. They registered all their regular customers to ensure they received their provisions and refused to serve casual customers. In their defence a registration system had been suggested by the Food Controller. What caused hostility and exacerbated the situation however was that the proprietor was Edwin Oakley, a three-time former Mayor, serving Alderman and member of the Food Control Committee, who had strenuously defended shopkeepers during Committee meetings.

Accusations of profiteering and double standards within the food distribution system became commonplace. The working class in the town could only see a bitter division developing between those who were fighting for their country and those who had stayed at home and were reaping the rewards and it was clear that confrontation was inevitable.

Matters came to a head in late January 1918 when on the 22nd the Trades and Labour Council sent a letter to the Town Clerk. In it they requested the reorganisation of the Food Control Committee to include six labour members including two women. They stated their reasons and those of the general public, being a total mistrust and suspicion of the Committee, comprising as it did members directly involved in the provisions trade, a clear reference to Oakley. The letter went before the

The Town Hall Council Chamber photographed in 1907. On the walls hang portraits of former Mayors. Few photographs exist of the interior rooms of the Town Hall.

T. G. Hobbs/Source: Luton Museum Service

Town Council at their next meeting causing some stormy discussion and division among them. Eventually a motion was carried that the Council reply to the Trades and Labour Council that there was only one vacancy.

Mobilised by their Trades Unions almost all the workforce involved in engineering and munitions, nearly seven thousand people, assembled at the Moor at 9.00am on Monday, 28th January and made their way to the Town Hall. A deputation from the Trades and Labour Council met the Food Control Committee in the Council Chamber. Chairman John Staddon told the deputation that all members of the Committee were present with the exception of Oakley, who was in London on business!

Members of the deputation stated the various grievances that had come to their attention. They had, they said, reached the stage where there was now no alternative but to act in the interest of the majority of townspeople, something that the Food Committee had failed to do. The mass walkout was the result. The decision had not been taken lightly but the Committee had brought it upon themselves. There was an overriding sense of inequality between the classes and a feeling of disgust at the way the situation had been allowed to develop.

Staddon told the deputation that the Committee agreed there were a number of problems to be addressed but criticised the Food Ministry over their general handling of the food situation. The deputation listened politely but told the Food Committee that excuses were of no concern to them. They then presented a resolution setting out three demands.

If the constitution for the Food Committee remained at twelve, they were to have a representation of four Labour members including one woman. If the number was increased to fifteen, (something that Lord Rhondda was then considering), the representation was to be six, two of whom would be women. Further to this, there was to be a total abolition of private deliveries except where they were considered essential. Finally, the Trades and Labour Council demanded the removal of Alderman Oakley from the Food Committee.

The deputation reiterated that these were no longer requests, they were demands. The outcome of the dispute was simple and an answer was required by the end of the day. If the demands were met everyone would return to work, if not, the stoppage would continue. Outside, they continued, were nearly seven thousand workers who, together with their dependants, probably represented nearly fifty thousand or the vast majority of the population of Luton. As far as the Trades and

Labour Council were concerned, the Food Committee were responsible for the walkout and it was up to them to sort it out.

The Town Clerk made little impression upon the deputation when he stated that the Food Committee had no powers to make appointments and the matter would have to be put before the full Council. That, they said, was not their problem and did not alter the fact that an immediate answer was required. The Trades and Labour Council had essentially presented the Food Committee with a fait accompli.

Staddon saw that a prolonged dispute with the suspension of vital war work was something that the town certainly did not want, attracting, as it surely would, national interest. In what was essentially the only way out of the predicament, albeit with the backing of his Committee, Staddon told the Trades and Labour Council that provided they would accept three as opposed to four members on a committee of twelve, he would guarantee that their demands would be met and at the same time pledged the agreement of the Town Council. He could not say who would resign but was prepared to put himself forward to help resolve any problems. As for Alderman Oakley, Staddon felt that his position on the Food Committee had become untenable after all the criticism directed at him and was certain he would offer his resignation.

The Trade and Labour Council deputation accepted the proposal and guarantees from Staddon and thanked the Food Committee for the hearing. They offered Staddon the opportunity to speak to the workers who by now had returned to the Moor. The mass meeting listened to members of the deputation outline the talks that had occurred and, to great applause, the guarantees that had been given. Staddon gave the assurances that the Food Committee was working on their behalf and although there were a number of dissenting voices and some heckling the overwhelming majority voted for an immediate return to work.

The following evening, Tuesday, the Town Council met in what was, up to that time, probably the most vociferous and acerbic session to be held in the history of the Council. Staddon opened the meeting with an outline of the events that had taken place the previous day, describing how the Food Committee had been faced with an alarming decision. It was pointless, he said, to look back on what had or had not been said or done. It had to be recognised that the town had a huge working class population and therefore it was in the interest of everybody to settle the dispute immediately. On this basis therefore he had made the offer of the three places on the committee to the Trades and Labour

Council. Staddon then moved the adoption of the Food Committee recommendations, which was seconded.

For nearly three hours these recommendations were the subject of heated debate and at times caustic comment. The Councillors who sat on the Food Committee were obviously behind Staddon as were a number of others but many voices were raised in dissent. There was particular objection to the idea that the Council should be seen to accede to the demands of the Labour group and that the guarantees had been given by the 'paltry Food Committee' as one Councillor described them. Staddon was singled out for a personal verbal attack by Councillor Briggs who commented that although it was clear that the Deputy Mayor had many of his colleagues in his pocket, it was not for him to make decisions for others.

Alderman Oakley, as predicted by Staddon, offered his resignation from the Food Committee and said, in a biting short speech, that not having wished to be selected in the first place, nothing would give him greater pleasure than to resign. In a sharp attack on the Trades and Labour Council he hoped that those who were selected to go on the Committee were stronger than their first member because an old woman would have done a better job than he did. Oakley also hoped that the town and the 'best townspeople' would give him the credit for not serving for his own interest.

Oakley's resignation was accepted but another was required. At one point it was suggested that the Food Committee resign en masse and then re-elect but the Town Clerk suggested this was a rather undignified procedure for a Council Committee. Eventually Councillor Bone, the only Labour supporter on the Town Council, offered his resignation which was gratefully accepted.

At the end of the meeting Staddon made another statement. He had listened to the debate with an amount of pain, he said. Thanking those members that had supported him, he paid tribute to Oakley and Bone for their work on the Committee. With regard to accusations made against members of the Food Committee he said that no trace could be found of any specific charge but hoped that everyone would now settle down and not indulge in any recriminations.

The motion, that three members of the Labour Party should be elected to the Food Committee, was moved and carried unanimously.

The three representatives took up their positions shortly afterwards and there was to be no further confrontation. The problems over food supply had, however, created a wide gulf between working class Lutonians and their Town Council which had not existed at any time in the past and a deep sense of suspicion of the Council's actions remained.

What also remained were the food queues. On 7th April 1918 Lord Rhondda introduced meat rationing through a coupon system and in May, using registration cards, tea, butter and sugar followed. Rationing would not finally be lifted until November 1920.

The war had also brought about a new spirit among servicemen who were determined to make sure that they did not allow themselves to become Britain's forgotten citizens who were thrown on the scrap heap having served their useful purpose for the country. They saw during the years of war, injustices, administrative blunders, muddle in recruitment, unsatisfactory training of disabled men and bureaucratic delays in the implementation of Pensions.

The result was the birth of the ex-servicemen's movement. Organisations catering for servicemen, their families, widows and children had existed for many years but for the first time discharged soldiers and sailors were organised into societies that now demanded from the state as their right, what had been given as charity in the past, and only then if they were lucky.

The first of the societies to acquire national status was the NATIONAL ASSOCIATION of DISCHARGED SAILORS and SOLDIERS which grew out of a meeting held in Blackburn in September 1916 and affiliated itself with both the growing Labour and Trade Union movements. The Association was quickly followed by the NATIONAL FEDERATION of DISCHARGED and DEMOBILISED SAILORS and SOLDIERS. The Federation had its origins in April 1917 when the Liberal MP for East Edinburgh, James Myles Hogge, sponsored a meeting at the National Liberal Club and within a few months a number of local branches had been formed. It was no surprise therefore that the Federation wore the colours of the Liberal party. Hogge however was a radical and a rebel who had voted numerous times against Lloyd George's Coalition as well as Asquith's Liberal government and his tone would influence the Federation's political position in its formative years.

If the Federation was the younger of the two societies it quickly became the stronger, more powerful and more broadly representative of all four nations of the British Isles, except in one area. It barred from its membership all officers, apart from those who had been commissioned from the ranks. This strong anti-officer bias was to remain a stigma during the Federation's early years.

The Federation owed much of its early growth and development to a Bill, that had its second reading in the House of Commons in March 1917. The Military Service (Review of Exemptions) Act, provided for the medical re-examination of discharged, disabled men with a view to possible further service in the armed forces. The Act was highly controversial and the rigidity with which it was implemented did not help, based as it was on the premise that if a man was able to make his living in civilian life he could be re-employed somewhere in the army.

The storm of protest around the country and within Parliament itself was so great that in July 1917 a Select Committee of the House of Commons was appointed to investigate the working of the Act which resulted in a radical change in the recruiting system. The Federation under the leadership of Hogge was especially vociferous in their protest and the campaign waged by them was so vigorous that it led to the formation of a third ex-servicemen's society, the COMRADES of the GREAT WAR.

The birth of the third organisation resulted from a letter sent to the press in July 1917 by a Conservative MP, Lieutenant Colonel Sir John Norton-Griffiths. In the letter he expressed his view that extremists were trying to hijack discharged servicemen for this own political ends, an obvious reference to Hogge, and that to counter this propaganda the ex-servicemen should work together for the good of the country by keeping well clear of politics. Otherwise, Norton-Griffiths feared, the country would be faced by growing discontent to the point of revolution. Together with his letter Norton-Griffiths sought the unofficial blessing of the Secretary of State for War in forming another ex-servicemen's society. Lord Derby, who had succeeded Kitchener, not only gave his blessing but also presided over a conference on 1st August 1917 at which a constitution was discussed. Here Norton-Griffiths' perceived view of a non-political organisation was challenged by another Conservative MP, Colonel Wilfred Ashley, who put forward the proposal that the executive committee of the new society should include members of both Houses of Commons and Lords.

A letter appeared in The Times in late August launching the Comrades and it was apparent that Ashley's view had prevailed, as two-thirds of the new society's executive committee consisted of MPs. An inaugural meeting was held on 13th November 1917 at the Mansion

House, London, which was attended by many distinguished figures among whom were the newspaper proprietors Lords Beaverbrook and Rothermere and Field Marshall Lord French. Money raised at the meeting amounted to the then substantial sum of £35,000 and so the Comrades were launched with powerful backers and ample funds.

Things did not go well for the Comrades however with membership figures very poor, mainly due it was felt to the committee's composition of MPs and officers, thus vindicating John Norton-Griffiths' idea of a non-political society. Lord Derby, realising the need for the Comrades to appeal more to the discharged men, acted quickly to appoint a leading personality to the position of Chairman of the General Committee of the Comrades. Captain E. E. B. Towse VC was a hero of the Boer War during which he had not only won his decoration but had also been permanently blinded whilst serving with the Gordon Highlanders. It was a brilliant move by Lord Derby and under the leadership of Towse the Comrades flourished and presented a real challenge to the Federation's dominance.

The autumn of 1917 therefore saw three rival organisations representing ex-servicemen, each with their own party political connections, eyeing each other with suspicion, envy and at times bitterness and vying with each other to become the masters of the ex-servicemen's movement.

In April 1917 a branch of the Federation was formed in the town making it one of the first. Its full title was the Luton and District Discharged Sailors and Soldiers Association but to make things easier for all concerned the branch always referred to itself as the DS&S and took its parent organisation's badge, an ivy leaf. Operating initially from an office at 15 Castle Street, early expansion of the branch saw a move to bigger premises a 3 Church Street.

The Luton branch of the Comrades of the Great War was formed in November 1917, their badge being a Union Jack, and as with the Federation it was one of the first constituted. With very few funds initially the Comrades held their early meetings in the Town Hall.

In January 1918 the DS&S were reporting a local membership of one hundred and eighty-one against that of the Comrades' forty-two and the bitterness and animosity of the two societies was very much in evidence between the two local branches and more particularly

Members of the Luton and District Discharged Sailors and Soldiers Association march with their banner. Formed in April 1917 the DS&S competed with the Comrades of the Great War to be the senior ex-servicemen's organisation in Luton. The rivalry was often bitter. Source: Luton Museum Service

from the DS&S. At a meeting prior to forming a Dunstable branch the Luton branch chairman H. W. Booth spoke at length on the formation of the Federation and on how the Comrades had been formed to 'cripple their influence', as the Federation was seen as a thorn in the side of the authorities and that the Comrades' sole purpose was to 'bust the Federation'. Booth also spoke of the Comrades' political affiliation to the Conservative party and made the point that the Federation were non-political. (The DS&S went out of their way to claim no political bias. Even their letterheads contained the phrases non-party and non-sectarian which was certainly stretching the truth somewhat.) The DS&S also formed a propaganda committee to oversee various recruitment drives and at the same time to try and discredit the Comrades. At their first annual meeting in April 1918 Booth announced the branch had over three hundred members and was growing rapidly.

Both societies were also engaged in looking for premises large enough to have recreational facilities for their members as well as administrative offices. The Comrades were first and established their memorial club and institute at 5 Upper George Street. The club was formally opened on the 20th July 1918 by their chairman Captain Towse who was accompanied by the Mayor Charles Dillingham and other dignitaries. After a tour of the premises a reception was held in

The Ivy Leaf club in Park Street, headquarters of the DS&S. Previously it had been the home of the Third Volunteer Battalion of the Bedfordshire Regiment.

Source: Luton Central Library

the Town Hall assembly room.

Unfortunately the DS&S took exception to certain comments made by the Mayor at the opening ceremony when he referred to the Comrades as a non-political organisation. Many of the DS&S members were upset that the Mayor was inferring that they were political (which of course they were) and the row was only ended when Mayor Dillingham made a statement denying emphatically that he intended any slur on the DS&S. Once again though it was clear that political affiliation was a touchy subject.

In November 1918 the DS&S moved their headquarters to larger premises. These were established in the building that had previously been the headquarters of the volunteer battalion of the Bedfordshire Regiment on the corner of Park Street and Lea Road and was named the Ivy Leaf Club

In July 1918 the Town Council was approached by the Army Council who requested the loan of William Smith, the Town Clerk. They required him to act as secretary to the newly-formed Central Council of Supplies. An extraordinary Council meeting was called to consider the request. After a rather stormy debate it was agreed by a small majority to let Smith take up the post on the proviso that he would still carry on with his Council duties whenever possible. Flattered by the Army's interest in his abilities Smith considered the appointment but turned it down. He felt that he could not do justice to either position with the workload required and his duty lay with Luton and the Council. They breathed a collective sigh of relief at Smith's decision.

Substantial advances through the summer of 1918 were the first tangible signs that the tide of war was swinging towards the Allies and on Monday 11th November 1918 the Armistice was declared. David Lloyd George decided to call an early general election. The formation of the Coalition Government had split the Liberal party into two factions, the Lloyd Georgists and the Asquithians. Supporters now hoped that the Prime Minister would reunite the party and fight the election alongside Asquith. Hopes were dashed however when Lloyd George announced at a Liberal rally that he would stand under a joint manifesto with Bonar Law, leader of the Coalition Conservatives. Labour members were invited to join but the Party decided to fight the election independently.

Official recognition of Coalition candidates was given in the form of a controversial letter signed by both Lloyd George and Bonar Law and those Liberals amenable to the Coalition received it. The letter was sarcastically dubbed 'the Coupon' by Asquith, a direct reference to wartime rationing. The 1918 general election would always be known as the 'Coupon election'.

Sensing that the popular feeling in the country was for revenge, Lloyd George conducted his campaign

Cecil Harmsworth,
Liberal MP for Luton 1911-1922.
F. Thurston/Source: Luton Museum Service

speeches in a similar vain. He urged that Britain 'should extract the last penny we can get out of Germany' and to make them pay for the war 'until the lemon pips squeak'. A different mood entered a speech that he made on 24th November when he said 'What is our task? To make Britain a country fit for heroes to live in.

The country responded by returning the Coalition with a landslide victory with over four hundred and seventy seats. Labour made substantial advances in taking sixty seats but Asquith's Liberals were decimated and only thirty were returned. The election was not all good news however. Even though women over the age of thirty were given the vote for the first time the electorate turnout was only fifty-nine percent. Similarly, the armed forces had been given two weeks to vote, (the election was held on 14th December and the result declared on the 28th), but it was estimated that only one in four had bothered to take part

In Luton Cecil Harmsworth held the 'coupon' as the Coalition Liberal candidate. Returned with a big majority he was appointed to the position of Under Foreign Secretary. His only opponent, Willet Ball, stood as the town's first Labour candidate.

November was also time for the annual selection of the Mayor of Luton. The person elected was normally one of the longer-serving members of the Town Council who, during their year of office, also took on the role of Chief Magistrate. They also had to be able to finance the expenses that the position incurred. Seven members of the Council had already served terms as Mayor, sometimes more than once.

Two nominations had been put forward at a meeting of the Council on 8th September 1918. An extremely close vote of eleven to ten with one paper left blank saw Councillor Henry Impey elected to serve as Mayor for the forthcoming year, beating Councillor Arthur Attwood. On the 9th November the public of Luton turned out to celebrate its annual Mayoral day. Anticipating the possibility of an announcement of peace or news that Germany had signed the Armistice, a large than normal crowd had gathered expectantly in front of the Town Hall.

Promptly at midday the Council with the exception of Councillors Staddon and Hubbard assembled at the foot of the Town Hall steps. The retiring Mayor, Charles Dillingham, invited the nominating Councillor Charles Yarrow to read out a resume of the new incumbent's career. After Yarrow had finished Dillingham read the Council's official resolution `That Henry Impey Esquire of Whitecroft, London Road, Luton, a Councillor of the Borough, be and he is, hereby elected Mayor of the Borough of Luton for the ensuing year'. To generous applause from the crowd Dillingham declared the resolution unanimously carried.

Henry Impey had been born in Luton in 1865 and had the benefit of a good education. At the age of sixteen Impey secured a position with the Council as a junior in the Borough Surveyor's Office beating forty-five other applicants for the post. Having served over eight years in the department the opportunity arose to move to the position of Sanitary Inspector. This new post gave Impey more freedom, for he had found desk work to be rather tedious. He stayed in the job for the next four years during which time he was also appointed Drainage and Building Inspector.

Henry Impey, Mayor of Luton, November 1918 to November 1919. Luton born, he had served the town for seventeen years as a hard-working Councillor.
Source: Luton Central Library

In 1894 Impey left the Corporation's employment and established himself in private business as an estate agent and surveyor, initially in partnership with a well-known local businessman, Henry Sell. Animosity and disagreement led to the break up of their firm after only a few years but each carried on in separate business, Impey working from premises in Castle Street. He had by this time built up a lot of business acumen including ownership of a number of properties, the rent from which provided the majority of his income.

In November 1902 Impey was elected to the Town Council for the first time as a member for the East Ward, which he would represent continuously for the next seventeen years. He became one of the Corporation's most active and conscientious members serving on the many Committees and having an excellent attendance record at Council meetings. He also served as a member of the Bedfordshire County Council for a number of years prior to the war.

Throughout his life Impey had been a stalwart member of the Mount Tabor Primitive Methodist Church. As a young man he had been active in the Sunday school and worked hard in promoting the work of the Church before he was appointed its Superintendent. He also became a lay preacher, a role that saw him travel throughout the country.

In 1897 having been instrumental in the raising of funds, Impey laid the foundation stone for a new Church building in London Road which replaced the corrugated iron structure in Hibbert Street that had served the Methodists for a number of years.

Impey was a well respected and popular Councillor both with his colleagues and the people of Luton. Regarded as a man who persevered with a cause he believed in, he was also thought of as someone who liked to have his own way. Now he had been given the highest accolade, representing his home town as its Chief Officer, and he looked forward to his year in office.

In his proposal speech for Impey however, Councillor Yarrow was to speak some prophetic words. 'We *are entering on the most eventful year the town has ever experienced, an epoch in our history.*'.

With the signing of the Armistice the demobilisation of the British Armed Forces was put into operation. As early as January 1915 a report had been prepared finalising the practical arrangements and in the summer of 1916 a demobilisation sub committee was formed. In August 1917 a master plan was established by the War Office, Admiralty and Air Ministry in conjunction with the Ministry of Labour with a basic objective of averting mass unemployment. To this end the break up of the forces was to be done by individuals rather than by units. The first releases were made up of anyone who could prove they were from indispensable civilian employment or that they had a job to go to on production of a signed affidavit from an employer. Only ten percent of the early releases were to be made up of long serving men. Twenty-six dispersal stations were set up, one for each regimental district and twenty thousand soldiers were employed in the clerical side of the operation.

Demobilisation began on 9th December, nearly a month after the Armistice. Each man was sent to a camp behind lines from where he proceeded to his allocated dispersal station. It took twenty-four hours to complete formalities and each man then left with civilian clothes, twenty-eight days' pay and ration allowance, twenty-eight days' leave, a railway warrant, ration book and an out-of-work donation policy. (The policy entitled the ex-servicemen to benefits to a maximum of twenty weeks.) At the end of the leave period the serviceman was technically demobilised.

The scheme had worthy intentions but was totally inadequate and misguided in two respects, that of the provision of employment, which put the onus on employers, and also from the outset it was simply not quick enough. (In February 1920, one hundred and twenty-five thousand men still awaited demobilisation.) The deficiencies of the plan finally spilled over into serious unrest within the army camps.

In November 1918 men from Addington rest camp sent a telegraph to the King informing him that they intended to burn down Buckingham Palace. They had served in Mesopotamia for two years without leave and had, had no pay for nine months. The granting of Christmas leave to the men prevented things going any further. On the 3rd January 1919 came more trouble. Ten thousand unarmed men marched into the centre of Folkestone but returned to camp when promised seven days' leave. On learning the following day that they had been ordered to France they marched on the town again, this time fully armed. The War Office immediately reinstated the leave and the men returned peaceably to their camp. The following day at Dover two thousand men demonstrated in the town centre. A deputation met with the Mayor in the Dover Guildhall while outside the soldiers entertained themselves by singing popular songs to piano accompaniment before the men returned to camp peaceably. On the 6th January eight thousand servicemen held a mass meeting at Brighton.

Another incident occurred on 8th February when three thousand armed soldiers marched on Horse Guards Parade. They were due to return to France after four months' leave and their grievance concerned a lack of food for them while waiting to embark from Victoria station. The men were escorted back to the station peaceably by sections of the home garrison.

Even though these demonstrations had been non-violent and the granting of periods of leave had a pacifying effect, the Government made changes to ensure there was no further trouble. Lloyd George appointed Winston Churchill to oversee the demobilisation programme and he immediately set about reorganising it on the basis of first in, first out. An increase in pay was also given to those troops on occupation duty in Germany. These changes had the desired result and there was no further unrest or demonstrations . . . within the armed forces.

As 1919 dawned an overwhelming desire to get back to normal was uppermost in people's thoughts. Peace however had still to be declared and in anticipation of this a provisional date of the 4th August, Bank Holiday Monday, and the anniversary of the outbreak of war, was set aside as the National day of Peace Celebrations.

The Build Up
To Peace Day
January-July 1919

Town Council meetings were always held bi-weekly at 6.00pm on a Tuesday in the Town Hall Council Chamber. During the early months of 1919 three subjects took up much of the Council's' time — the future of the Town Hall buildings, proposals for the use of War-down House and Park and the Peace Day programme.

The Town Hall was by now beginning to fall into a bad state of repair particularly on the Manchester Street side of the building. It was estimated by the Tolls and Municipal Buildings Committee that £2,000 would need to be spent on improvements. The Council debated on the need to spend money on the existing building or to consider proposals for new municipal buildings. There was no doubt that the majority of Councillors felt the present building had, had its day. Alderman Wilkinson summed it up. If they (the Council) could show him another town of sixty thousand inhabitants with a Town Hall that looked as cheap and so unpretentious as theirs, he would like to know it because he had not seen it.

A resolution was passed that plans should be prepared for new buildings and the Council could then decide whether or not to carry them out. It soon became apparent that the new building would be a non-starter. The Tolls and Municipal Buildings Committee reported back that first estimates of the cost would be £150,000 minimum, a figure well beyond the budget of the Council especially considering that only eight years previously £50,000 had been put forward as a proposed cost.

The overall feeling was that a new Town Hall was out of the question for another ten of fifteen years. Improvements would therefore have to be made to the existing building including reconstruction of offices, improved access and the provision of conveniences. It was felt that with these improvements the building could be utilised for a further twenty years although this was by no means a unanimous opinion.

Wardown House and Park had been purchased by the Town Council in 1905 and become Luton's premier recreational facility. For all of its popularity though, no real used could be found for the house even though for some time it had been used as a restaurant and during the war, as has already been referred to, a convalescent hospital.

In January 1919 proposals were being discussed in Council meetings for the provision of a maternity home in the town. It was agreed to appoint a Committee, the Maternity and Child Welfare, and passed a resolution to investigate using Wardown House and Park. They reported back to the full Council on 18th February. There was some measure of support for the scheme notably from the Luton Women's Labour Party but Lutonians in general were voicing a lot of opposition to what they considered to be the loss of their premier public park. Indeed the Councillors themselves were divided on the issue even though the need for a maternity home was not in doubt. After a heated debate it was agreed to postpone any decision to give time to look at alternative sites.

Over the next couple of months opposition to the scheme increased rapidly led by one of the local newspapers, the Luton News, which published a list of the Councillors' names who were in favour of or against the proposal and also voiced its opposition in its editorials. The campaign had an effect and the Maternity and Child Welfare Committee reported back at the Council meeting on 20th May that '*the Committee again fully discussed the question of utilising Wardown house for a Maternity home, and resolved to recommend that having regard to the hostility to the proposal . . . the Council abandon the proposal and rescind their resolution*'. After a short debate the committee's recommendation was approved, Mayor Impey expressing the opinion that they were taking a step in the best interest of the public.

Wardown House and Park had been saved for the town but the fact that the Council were prepared to discuss utilising it for other purposes only helped to distance them even further from the townspeople they represented.

The initial proposals for the Peace Day Celebrations were discussed by the full Council at their meeting of the 18th February 1919. Under the chairmanship of the Mayor, a Peace Celebrations Committee had been formed and their initial recommendations were reported back by Impey to his colleagues. They included a procession, decoration and illumination of the Town Hall and Corn Exchange, illumination of Wardown lake, a fireworks display, concerts, sports, a subscription banquet and a souvenir for the town's school children.

The issue that caused most debate among the Councillors was the manner in which the celebrations were to be financed. The Peace Committee felt that the expenditure should come from public funds and recommended that the Council raise a sum of £500 through the addition of a halfpenny to the rates, with £100 for the fireworks display to be raised by private subscription.

The Deputy Mayor, Councillor Dillingham, suggested that the whole cost should be met by private subscription, pointing out that £500 was nothing to a town the size of Luton and he was supported by Councillors Briggs and Hubbard. They raised an amendment to the recommendations but it was only supported by Councillor Unwin and the Peace Committee's report was adopted. It was summed up by Alderman Wilkinson who said that all sections of the community were catered by the Committee's 'nice modest programme'.

By April the two ex-servicemen's organisations were still waiting to hear what part they were to take in the celebrations and on the 29th the General Secretary of the DS&S. Henry Charles Cooper contacted the Town Clerk to ascertain why they had not received any details.

In response, William Smith sent a letter to the DS&S and the Comrades organisations the following day. Outlining the proposals already approved by the Council, the letter continued:

In response, William Smith sent a letter to the DS&S and the Comrades organisations the following day. Outlining the proposals already approved by the Council, the letter continued:

'It is intended that the Procession shall comprise representatives of various Works, workers and organisations connected with the war, including men who have served in the Navy, Army and Air Force and War Prisoners. The numbers of these men provisionally agreed upon are as under:

Navy...48 & 4 off   Air Force...48
Army...49 & 8 off   War Prisoners...48
and the committee have decided to invite your Association to

Wardown House. Built in 1877 for Frank Chapman Scargill, Chairman of the Board of Health, the house and estate were originally named Bramingham Shott. Purchased by the Council the grounds were opened to the public in 1905. Wardown would be at the centre of much of the controversy in 1919. Source: Luton Museum Service

submit the names of the following number of such men to form part of the procession:

Navy...12	*Air Force...12*
Army...24	*War Prisoners...12*

The men who are chosen must have been living in Luton when they joined up, and their names should be sent to me by 31st May.

My Committee are not prepared to incur any expense in connection with the attendance of any person in the procession.

If you have any suggestions or proposals to make regarding the Celebration programme, perhaps you would kindly write to me.

Yours faithfully,
W. SMITH,
Town Clerk.

The DS&S had by now become established as the premier ex-servicemen's organisation within the town and had a paying membership of nearly one thousand five hundred. In May 1919 it launched it own bi-weekly magazine, the DS&S Journal. The Comrades could boast a larger membership of nearly two thousand but they were not as well organised. Even so, the majority of ex-servicemen remained unaffiliated to either society. Much of the DS&S success was down to their General Secretary, Henry Charles Cooper. A former army captain Cooper had been discharged after being badly wounded and although he suffered bouts of poor health he had worked tirelessly for the organisation since its formation. It was Cooper who in response to the letter from Smith led a deputation from the DS&S Henry Impey on the 6th May to discuss the peace proposals more fully. The DS&S had particular concern over the number of ex-servicemen required to participate in the procession and felt very strongly that the number should be much greater. They also considered the one day programme rather mean taking into consideration that three days had provisionally been set aside for celebrations. Cooper therefore suggested to Impey a proposal for a Drumhead Memorial Service, an idea initially discussed at the DS&S annual general meeting in January. The service would honour those who had given their lives in the war.

Henry Charles Cooper, Secretary of the Luton branch of the Federation, the DS&S. Cooper was involved in all the negotiations with the Council over Peace Day celebrations and had a far higher profile than the secretary of the Comrades.
Source: Luton Museum Service

The Luton Free Church Council met on 16th May at which similar ideas to the DS&S were discussed. They appointed 'a *Committee to confer with the Mayor with a view to arranging a great united demonstration to celebrate the conclusion of peace ... such a demonstration to be held in some public place in the open air'.*

Impey conveyed the DS&S proposals to the Council at their next meeting who agreed to increase the number of participating ex-servicemen. In the meantime the executive committee of the DS&S reviewed their meeting with the Mayor and on 18th May Cooper wrote to Impey:

To his Worship the Mayor (councillor H. Impey).

Dear Sir,

Advertising to the matter of Local Peace Celebrations in connection with which a deputation from this Association had the honour to wait upon you on May 6th, I am directed by my Committee to place before you for consideration the following suggestions.

We propose that in view of the fact that there are approx. 4,000 discharged and demobilised men in the town, arrangements be made for at least 800 men to take part in the proposed procession.

We also suggest that Peace Celebrations be spread over two days, and that the second day be devoted to the entertainment of the ex-service and serving men in the town.

Attached to this letter is our suggested programme for the second day.

Assuming that the Peace Celebrations will take place on August 4th and 5th we propose that a Special Memorial Service be organised in the form of a Drumhead Service, with the massed choirs and combined clergy of the town. We, as Discharged, Disabled men, will be to the fore in our willingness to assist in the organisation of this proposition.

I am further directed to ask you to be good enough to furnish my Committee with your detailed programme of the Celebrations, and trust that you will be able to comply with that request as we are anxious to assist where possible.

I have the honour to be, Sir,
Yours faithfully,
H. CHAS. COOPER, Secretary

The programme for the second day suggested that the ex-servicemen assemble at the Moor for 1.30pm and then take part in a procession and march past to Luton Hoo for the Memorial Service, followed by sports and refreshments and culminating in a fireworks display and torchlight procession.

In response to their letter the DS&S received the following reply from the Town Clerk:

Dear Sir,
Your letter of 18th May to the Mayor has been placed before my

Committee, who have directed me to state that they are willing to increase to 200 (instead of 96) the number of representatives of the Army in the proposed procession on Peace Day and to ask your Association and the Comrades of the Great War to each submit the names of 75 (instead of 24) of such men. The Committee do not feel able to adopt any of your other suggestions, and have asked me to state that the money at their disposal is very limited and will be barely sufficient for carrying out their limited programme.

The Committee see no reason for giving a second fireworks display, as there will be one on the day appointed for the Celebrations.

Yours faithfully,

W. SMITH

Town Clerk

The DS&S Committee were extremely unhappy with the tone of the letter and attitude of the Council towards the ex-servicemen. They felt that the men who had fought to achieve peace were now being snubbed and the question of the Council not having enough money to fund greater participation in the Celebrations an insult. Extra money they believed could be utilised from various funds subscribed to during the war and which now lay dormant. Through their journal they appealed to the public for their support at a time of rejoicing and for Luton to set an example in celebrating peace and not to lag behind.

At their general meeting on 24th May, the DS&S announced that it would hold its own Drumhead Service on Sunday 3rd August at Luton Hoo Park subject to permission from Lady Wernher, the Lady of the Manor and owner of the Hoo, to be attended by representative Clergy of all Denominations and following a procession through the town's main streets accompanied by massed bands.

The Council now came in for criticism on another aspect of their celebration plans from another source, the local press. Provisional details had suggested that six hundred schoolchildren representing all the Luton schools would take part in the procession. Editorials in local papers questioned the practicality of the plan. As the official Peace days were scheduled for August and schools were on their summer break who would organise and supervise the children considering that many staff could well be away on holiday? Would it not therefore be more sensible to consider a special day of celebrations for the children?

The criticism obviously had some effect. On 3rd June the full Council met to give formal approval to the programme of Peace Celebrations subject to one or two items being given further consideration. One of these was the provision of a special day to be set aside for a party to entertain the town's children. The suggestion caused considerable debate among the Councillors and finance reared its head again. Provisional estimates were of £700 required to cater for around ten thousand children and once again the Council was split over methods of funding. Alderman John Staddon believed funds should be made available for the children and also the ex-servicemen whom he considered the two sections of the public to have priority. Mayor Impey on the other hand felt catering for such numbers of children to be a major task and suggested divided groups with money raised from public subscription. No decision was taken by the Council but it was agreed to pursue the matter further.

The children were also unwittingly involved in another heatedly debated issue. This concerned the provision of a Commemoration Medal bearing the Borough arms and the inscription 'Borough of Luton Celebration of Peace on Conclusion of Great War 1914-1919 Henry Impey Mayor' to be given to each child, the cost of which had been estimated at £150. A number of Councillors felt the medal design was hardly worthy of the occasion and Alderman Staddon had felt so strongly that he had consulted his fellow directors at Messrs Vyse Sons & Co Ltd, a local hat manufacturer, who had readily agreed to provide medals for the children as well as to contribute an additional £100 above the original estimate.

It was no surprise therefore that Mayor Impey moved that the offer from Messes Vyse be accepted. This was seconded by Councillor Barford who through Alderman Staddon thanked the generosity of Messrs Vyse and also remarked how they had helped the Peace Committee out of the considerable difficulty over the question of finance which had faced them constantly in preparing the Peace programme.

On 27th June at the request of James Baker, the Steward of Luton Hoo, Impey spoke with Lady Wernher with regard to the celebrations. She wanted to ascertain if there was any way in which she could help. The result was the arrangement of a party for ex-servicemen, provisionally to be held at Luton Hoo Park on 16th August.

Peace was finally declared on Saturday 28th June and at 3.50pm Mayor Impey, accompanied by the Town Clerk, made the official proclamation from the balcony of the Town Hall to the large Crowd that had gathered in anticipation of the news. The evening however was marred by outbreaks of hooliganism in the town centre. The Red Cross Band who were to play for the crowd had only just begun performing when several youths threw fireworks amongst them causing damage to a number of instruments. Further fireworks were thrown and they eventually refused to continue with their performance. A number of crackers were thrown in front of horses and in one reported incident a 'cannon' type firework was placed in a young baby's pram slightly injuring the child. Other fireworks were thrown indiscriminately among the crowd. The whole evening left the majority of Lutonians with a feeling of disgust that a day of thanks should have been totally overshadowed by an outbreak of rowdyism.

For no apparent reason the official date for peace celebrations was now brought forward from early August and fixed for Saturday 19th July. The DS&S Executive Committee met on Monday 30th June at the Ivy Leaf Club and began with a minute's silence in memory of fallen comrades. A report was then presented by the chairman, Mr W. B.Clay, who with Mr S. J. Allison had acted as the branch delegates at the Whitsun Conference of the National Federation held in Manchester. The general feeling of the conference was that the Federation should take no part in Peace Celebrations until all discharged and demobilised men had been found employment. It was unanimously agreed therefore that the Luton branch should adhere to the decision and the opinion was expressed that it was unfortunate that the country could spend money on celebrations while men who had fought for the peace were searching in vain for work.

Another report was presented by Henry Charles Cooper and Harold Hoy the treasurer, with regard to a meeting they had attended with representatives of the local clergy, Ministers of all Denominations and the Red Cross Band. They had discussed the proposals for holding the special open-air drumhead memorial service. The Clergy had expressed a willingness to co-operate and the Rural Dean of Luton, Reverend A. E. Chapman, was to make arrangements for the service which would include massed choirs and bands. Cooper went on to report that the DS&S would take responsibility for organising the event including the procession arrangements. They would also be sending out an invitation to the Comrades of the Great War to participate. He finished the report by saying that it was hoped that the use of Wardown Park could be secured for the service and collections would be made on behalf of the Widows and Orphans Fund.

Why the DS&S now changed the proposed venue from Luton Hoo Park to Wardown is uncertain. There seems no reason why Lady Wernher would refuse use of the Park. It is more probable that Wardown was considered a more convenient and central location. However it is also possible that the suggestion was made by Impey in his discussions with the DS&S.

The Council met on 1st July and made available to the Peace Celebrations Committee the money raised from the halfpenny rate that had been levied. On July 4th the Committee was called together for a special meeting to finally consider their arrangements for Peace Day and the programme was agreed as follows:

❋ Decorations and flags to be displayed on the Town Hall, Corn Exchange, Public Library and Wardown House. The people of Luton were invited to decorate their homes, especially those on the route of the procession.

❋ The front of the Town Hall to be illuminated and single powerful electric lamps hung at the Corn Exchange and suspension bridge at Wardown lake.

❋ The procession from Luton Hoo to Wardown Park via Park Street, George Street and Manchester Street. The official car of the Council entitled 'Peace Enthroned' together with floats and theme cars supplied by local firms and contingents from various organisations and five bands.

❋ Six hundred school children to assemble at East Ward recreation ground (Manor Road) then to line up in Park Street and after witnessing the procession to join at the end. Twenty-four boys and twenty-four girls to represent the Modern School with equal numbers from the other schools. Girls provided with white sashes, hat bands for boys and rosettes for teachers.

❋ Afternoon events to take place at Wardown Park. Sports arranged on the cricket ground with a programme of eighteen events starting at 3.30pm together with tennis and bowls tournaments.

❋ The five bands from the procession to play at appointed places around the park during the afternoon and evening. Some entertainments and a funfair were still to be confirmed.

❋ Fireworks display to be held at the Northwest side of Popes Meadow commencing at 9.30pm and eight 'flares' situated at Hart Hill, London Road, the Downs and People's Park to be lit at 10pm.

It was also agreed that following incidents after the peace announcement the Town Clerk would issue a warning notice against the use of fireworks by the public in the streets or parks.

Two items were still outstanding, entertainment for the children and the Mayor's subscription banquet. With regard to the children the Council found themselves with problems over the delivery of the commemorative medals. Although they believed they had ordered them in good time the manufacturers Mappin and Webb could only guarantee 20th August as their earliest delivery date and it was not possible to present them until the schools had reassembled. It was therefore unanimously agreed to hold a children's day in late August or early September and it was left to the Mayor and Town Clerk to meet with teachers to make final arrangements. The question of funding was no longer considered a problem as there were already several offers of financial support.

The Mayor's subscription banquet was causing further headaches. Arranged as a male only dinner, Councillors, Council officers and friends of the Mayor were invited free while tickets were available for 'gentlemen' priced fifteen shillings. Tickets were made available to the ex-servicemen to purchase, which was again considered an insult. Strong claims were also put forward on behalf of women to be included in recognition of their work during the war. Nobody contested their claim but the difficulty appeared to be in where to hold the banquet to accommodate increased numbers. The Winter Assembly Hall was considered but dismissed as it would mean closing the swimming baths for two weeks. (The pool was boarded over in the winter months and, as the 'Winter Assembly Hall', was used for public dances and other events.) The Peace Committee appeared to pay no more than lip service to solving the problem and decided the banquet should remain all male and be held at the Plait Halls on the Monday 21st July. Some justification in their decision came from the fact that the Mayoress was entertaining ladies at a separate function and it was considered that this went much of the way in recognising their effort in the war.

The Town Clerk sent letters confirming the Peace programme to both the DS&S and the Comrades. Cooper contacted Impey with regard to the use of Wardown Park and was advised to put his request in writing. On the 5th July he sent the following two letters:

Re PEACE CELEBRATIONS   *July 5th 1919*

Dear Sir,

I have to acknowledge and thank you for your letter of the 3rd inst. re Peace Celebrations, and am directed to inform you that the National Federation of Discharged and Demobilised Sailors and Soldiers at their conference recently decided to take no part in Peace Celebrations as a protest against the unemployment existing amongst discharged and demobilised men and the inadequate compensation to widows and dependants.

This Association will therefore respectfully withdraw from the local peace rejoicing, having in view also the fact that our brothers are still fighting and dying for this country.

Yours faithfully,

For an on behalf of Luton and District Discharged Sailors and Soldiers Association

H. C. Cooper, Secretary

To the Town Clerk, Luton   *July 5th*

Dear Sir,

I am directed by my Committee to make application to the Council for the use of Wardown Park and bandstand on Sunday afternoon, July 20th, for a public drumhead memorial service.

His Worship the Mayor has expressed every sympathy with this object and instructed us to apply to you for the use of the Park. The service is being supported by all the clergy of the town, their choirs, and the bands of the town. I am also directed to extend a cordial invitation to the Mayor and Council to take part in the processions, which will be as follows:

2pm — Muster of serving and ex-servicemen (preceded by Mayor and Council, in the event of your accepting the invitation).

2.30pm — March to Wardown Park.

3pm — Drumhead memorial service.

I shall esteem it a favour if you will reply at your earliest in order to complete the final arrangements.

Yours faithfully,

H. C. Cooper

The full Council were not due to meet again until 22nd July. As the DS&S required an answer as quickly as possible the letter was placed before the Tolls and Public Buildings Committee who were meeting on the evening of 7th July. Six members also formed the majority of the Parks Committee who were responsible for Wardown. These members were asked by Smith if they would remain behind and discuss the request. This they did and decided to refuse the DS&S the use of Wardown Park. Two elements significantly influenced their decision.

The first concerned bye laws that had been passed in 1905 and in particular two clauses that were applicable to the use of the park.

Clause 27. A person shall not deliver a public address in any part of the pleasure ground. Provided that the foregoing prohibition shall not apply in any case where, upon application to the Council for permission to deliver any public address in the pleasure ground, upon such occasion or on such day and at such hour as shall be specified in such application, the Council may grant such permission subject to compliance with such conditions as they prescribe.

Clause 28. A person shall not play any musical instrument or sing in any part of the pleasure ground.

Under Clause 27 the Council had refused permission to organisations they considered only represented sectional interests. Permission was also required under Clause 28 to use the park's bandstand. It was agreed that the DS&S application was representative of only part of the ex-servicemen's movement. As there was no indication in their letter that the memorial service was a joint effort with the Comrades it was decided that approval for use of the park should not be given following the guidelines established by the Council.

The second problem that the Parks Committee members addressed was the relationship between the DS&S and the Comrades. During the war both organisations had tried in vain to seek the Mayor's patronage. The Committee members were therefore not prepared to compromise the Town Council with association to one ex-servicemen's organisation and not the other, believing that further bad feeling and jealousy would be the result. It was also felt inappropriate for the Mayor and Councillors to attend the memorial service for the same reasons.

The Town Clerk was instructed to offer the use of Popes Meadow or the Moor, both of which were considered suitable venues for the service. Later that evening the Parks Committee members' rejection of Wardown was reported to the Watch Committee who were also meeting and no objection was made with regard to the decision. (The

Watch Committee was responsible for the efficient running of the local police force.) On July 7th therefore, thirteen out of twenty-four Council members had become involved in the rejection of the use of Wardown.

The decision was conveyed to the DS&S in a letter from Smith:

DRUMHEAD MEMORIAL SERVICE: JULY 20th, 1919   July 8th
Dear Sir,

In reply to your letter of the 5th inst., I am empowered to authorise you to use either the Moor, New Bedford Road or Popes Meadow, Old Bedford Road, for drumhead memorial service on Sunday, July 20th, at 3pm, and shall be glad to learn as soon as possible which you may select. The Council are unable to permit you to use Wardown Park for the purpose.

The Council regret that it will not be practicable for them to take part in your procession.

Yours faithfully,
W. Smith
Town Clerk

Following receipt of the letter a meeting was urgently arranged between two members of the DS&S and the Mayor. Impey explained in detail the reasons behind the Council's rejection. The DS&S Executive Committee met to discuss the refusal and Cooper again wrote to Smith.

The Town Clerk   July 9th
Dear Sir,

With reference to your letter of yesterday's date containing the Council's refusal to sanction the use of Wardown Park for the drumhead memorial service arranged by this Association, and also the interview with the Mayor granted to two representatives of this Association.

It was stated that as a matter of principle the use of the Park could not be granted, as refusals had already been given to other societies.

I am directed to suggest that comparison between the objects for which other applications had been tendered for the use of the Park, and the memorial service, we submit, can in no sense be justified.

My Committee consider that Wardown Park, for reasons of organisation, etc., is the most public and suitable situation for the service and the refusal of the Council against the use of it for that purpose is very regrettable and totally unjustified.

My Committee wish me to say that a refusal by the Council was not contemplated, and we are surprised by the lack of sympathy expressed by their action, and trust that the Council were not biased by the fact that we are not officially taking part in the Peace Celebrations, the reasons for which you are no doubt fully aware.

The Committee making Wardown for their objective, have already made arrangements and had matter printed, etc., and I am directed to respectfully ask if the Council will see their way clear to reconsider the matter and grant this Association the use of the Park on Sunday, July 20th.

I am, Sir,

Yours faithfully,

H. C. Cooper

As far as Smith was concerned the decision was final and he sent the DS&S a curt reply.

July 10th

Dear Sir,

I have received your letter of the 9th inst., and will at once assure you that there is no lack of sympathy by the Council to the proposed drumhead memorial service, nor are they prejudiced in the matter because your Association have withdrawn from the official Peace celebration.

The decision not to permit you to hold the service in Wardown Park is definite and cannot be reconsidered.

Please therefore inform me, by the 11th inst., whether you wish to use either the Moor, New Bedford Road, or Popes Meadow, Old Bedford Road.

Yours faithfully,

W. SMITH

Town Clerk

Realising the Council were not going to change their minds the DS&S were forced to accept the decision.

Dear Sir,

I have to acknowledge receipt of your letter of date, and note that the Council's news, and at their further direction I will inform you before the 14th inst.

which place they select between the Moor and Popes Meadow.

Yours faithfully,

For an on behalf of Luton and District Discharged Sailors and Soldiers Association.

HY. CHAS. COOPER,

Secretary

The Council and the DS&S were now in a position of stalemate. The DS&S decided to pass its recent correspondence with the Town Clerk to the Luton News and this was duly published in its sister paper The Saturday Telegraph on 12th July. John Staddon also made it public that he was not happy with the decision arrived at by his colleagues. As front page news the dispute over Wardown was now brought into the open and to the attention of the public. At Luton Hoo it also attracted the interest of Lady Wernher.

Lady Alice Wernher had some sympathy with the DS&S cause having suffered the loss of her own son, Alex. Through her steward James Baker, she contacted their committee to offer the use of Luton Hoo park to stage their memorial service.

The DS&S had no hesitation in accepting her offer and at the same time they informed the Town Council that they would not be requiring the use of Popes Meadow or the Moor.

For the first time throughout the whole period of the Peace Day programme discussion the Comrades took action of their own. Their secretary Mr N. Shepherd wrote to the Town Clerk:

5, Upper George Street, Luton

15th July, 1919

Dear Sir,

Owing to the attitude that your Town Council has taken in refusing the local branch of the Discharged Sailors and Soldiers Federation request for the use of Wardown Park for a memorial service in honour and deep respect of our fallen comrades, the general committee of the local branch of the Comrades of the Great War have decided that this branch will respectfully

withdraw from the Peace procession that is to be held on
Saturday next.

Yours faithfully,
N. SHEPHERD
On behalf of the Comrades of the Great War
W. Smith Esq.
Town Clerk

The Comrades also sent a deputation to meet the DS&S to discuss the possibility of staging a counter-demonstration a short time after the Peace procession. the DS&S committee refused to get involved and the proposal went no further.

In the last few days before Peace Day ugly rumours began to circulate around the town. It was being said that if there was to be no memorial service at Wardown Park there would be no Mayoral banquet at the Plait Halls. Ironically the banquet was meeting with such little support towards the end of the week that it was reorganised on a smaller scale and the venue moved to the Town Hall assembly room.

At the Ivy Leaf Club, Cooper also heard rumours of impending trouble and that the DS&S were organising a counter procession. He arranged a meeting of his Executive Committee to discuss what action they could take. The result was an announcement inserted in *The Tuesday Telegraph* of 15th July. It disclaimed any intention of a counter- demonstration and also reiterated the decision taken nationally to refrain from taking any part in the celebrations and concluded with a executive committee appeal to all members to *`maintain order on peace day and so further the causes for which we are fighting so hard'.*

The rumours also came to the attention of the police. In charge of the Luton Borough force was Chief Constable Charles Griffin. Born at Olveston, Gloucestershire, Griffin was thirty-six years old and had been a serving officer for fifteen years in three police forces. He had been made Chief Constable of Clitheroe, Lancashire in 1914 before being appointed to the position at Luton ahead of fifty-three other applicants in May 1917.

Concerned with the possibility of trouble at a counter-demonstration he met with the DS&S executive committee to clarify their position and to advise them to instruct their members to keep order on Peace Day. The DS&S responded by inserting an announcement

LUTON AND DISTRICT

Discharged and Demobilised Sailors' and Soldiers' Association.

=================

"*Ivy Leaf*" *Club,*

Park Street, Luton,

July 3rd, 1919.

M...

....

Dear Sir,

In view of the fact the Peace Celebrations are being held on Saturday, July 19th, the date of our <u>Drum-head Memorial Service</u> has been fixed for Sunday, July 20th.

The Programme will be (for the procession):—Fall-in at Park Square, at 2.30; March to Wardown, where the Clergy and Choirs will await them; Service on arrival at Wardown.

Kindly let me know at your earliest, whether you will be able to be present.

Yours faithfully,

HY. CHAS. COOPER,
Secretary.

Invitation for the drumhead memorial service organised by the DS&S. Note the date July 3rd. The DS&S did not apply to the Town Council for permission to use Wardown Park until July 5th. Source: Luton Museum Serivce

75

of their disclaimer in the local press for a second time. On this occasion it was *The Saturday Telegraph* which for this one week was published on the Friday, 18th July. They also added a second announcement in much bolder type which was an *'appeal to Serving a Ex-Service men. The Chief Constable having made strong representations to the DS&S Association, my committee authorise me to issue a strong appeal to* ALL SERVING & EX-SERVICEMEN IN THE TOWN TOMORROW *to maintain a decorous order as soldiers and gentlemen, remembering that the children are looking forward to a perfect happy day. Remember the kiddies'.*

Charles Griffin, Chief Constable of the Luton Borough Police Force, May 1917 to May 1920. Pictured in his ceremonial uniform that he wore on the afternoon of Peace Day.
F. Thurston/Source: Luton Museum Service

One other announcement in the paper caught the eye. Headed JACK CORNWELL, BOY VC it asked for any naval men either on leave or demobilised who wished to take part in the Peace Procession to call and see Mr Strapps at the Rabbit public house in Old Bedford Road at 8.00pm, Friday, or in uniform at 1.30pm on Saturday. Charles Strapps the landlord was an ex-naval petty officer and also an active member of the Comrades. The tableau he had arranged to enter in the procession depicted sixteen year old John Travers Cornwell who had served aboard the light cruiser HMS Chester at the battle of Jutland on the 31st May 1916. With the rank of Boy First Class, Cornwell's duty had been to sight Chester's 5.5 inch forward gun. The cruiser had come under heavy fire and all the gun crew except Cornwell had been killed. Although severely wounded and under continuous fire he stood by his gun for more than fifteen minutes. Cornwell died of his wounds in hospital three days later but was awarded a posthumous Victoria Cross for his courage.

The stop press of *The Saturday Telegraph* also reported that final efforts had been made to get the discharged men's associations to take official part in the peace procession. In fact, negotiations had been in progress all of Friday. The DS&S stuck by their Federation's national decision to take no part but at the eleventh hour the Comrades were persuaded to be represented and advised the Peace Committee that a contingent of ex-servicemen and their band would take part in the procession. Their change of heart came about because they felt they still had to recognise and show their appreciation of the men who had fought for victory and Peace Day was to be the occasion to do it.

Peace Day arrived in Luton, and with it an undercurrent of high tension and bad feeling, fuelled by a money conscious and unbending Town Council and two ex-servicemen's organisations who were clearly unable to co-exist in the town without being suspicious and jealous of each other.

No one however was prepared for the events that were about to unfold.

The Riots
19th-21st
July 1919

The morning of Saturday July 19th dawned overcast and it was not long before rain began to fall. It did not prevent Lutonians of all ages gathering in large numbers along the Peace Procession route. At Luton Hoo Park various floats, emblematic cars and participating groups had been arriving throughout the morning. Under the leadership of Inspector Frederick Janes police officers were on duty to direct everyone to an allotted position which had been staked out and numbered.

Shortly after the scheduled start time of 2.00pm the procession began to move off from the park. Led by Chief Constable Griffin, dressed in ceremonial uniform and on horseback, acting as Chief Marshall for the event, accompanied by five other mounted policemen the procession slowly made its way along Park Street. Even though they had been last minute entries the Jack Cornwell tableau together with the contingent of Comrades ex-servicemen had been given the honour of leading the procession.

The six hundred schoolchildren had assembled on the East Ward recreation ground and now waited in Park Street cheering the procession as it passed by before joining it at the end. At the Ivy Leaf Club, DS&S members had gathered and strung a banner across the road proclaiming 'We do not want Processions, we want work'. As the Jack Cornwell tableau and the Comrades passed by there was an ill-mannered display of booing and shouts of abuse from their rivals. It was an isolated incident however, as the crowds lining both sides of the road responded to each entry with applause and cheers and spectators joined on at the rear of the procession as it passed them by.

The front of the procession reached the far end of George Street and turned through a right angle to pass directly in front of the

Town Hall where the Comrades ex-servicemen now halted and did a left turn to face the building. The Civic party led by Mayor Impey accompanied by members of the Council, the Town Clerk and the Mayor's Sergeant at Arms and Macebearer came down the steps of the Town Hall to the edge of the pavement to greet the ex-servicemen. Their appearance was a signal for a small number of people to start booing. The Comrades removed their boaters and hats and the Mayor proceeded to address them. He had, he said, received during the morning a Royal proclamation from the King that was to be read in the presence of men who had served in the armed forces. It expressed his Majesty's admiration of the courage and endurance displayed by the soldiers, sailors and airmen of the country during the past five years of war, His gratitude to all the brave men and women of the country for their devoted and patriotic service and His sympathy and that of the Queen with the relatives of the gallant men who have given their lives in their country's cause. Their Majesty's earnest hope was that the sick and wounded would be restored to good health. The proclamation concluded *'I rejoice with you today at the restoration of peace which I trust will bring to us all unity, contentment and prosperity'. Impey then continued with a personal message of his own 'to you men who have come into the procession today. The procession could not be complete without the representatives of the gallant men who have been fighting in the war, and therefore I desire most heartily to welcome you and trust that the outcome of our celebrations of peace, will be that peace will be inside and outside of our country for many years to come'.*

A noisy commotion broke out in the crowd at the bottom of Upper George Street. People began jeering the Mayor as he made his speech. It was countered by some sporadic cheering but this was drowned out by a further outburst of noisy booing.

The crowd quietened down as the Red Cross Band proceeded to play the National Anthem. With its completion the Comrades called for three cheers and in response one of the Councillors asked for three cheers for the ex-servicemen. This resulted in a resumption of jeering together with some abusive comments directed at Impey and the Councillors. The Civic party remained on the pavement as the procession moved on. It stopped a second time as the Council's official float 'Peace Enthroned' reached the Town Hall. It had been decided that the Royal proclamation should be read again to make the occasion more memorable for those who had contributed towards the cost of the float.

Peace Day 19th July 1919. Leading the Procession, the Jack Cornwell VC tableau followed by the Comrades Ex-servicemen approach Park Square, on their way to the Town Hall. Among the Naval ratings is George Heley who would later take part in the riot during the evening. The miserable wet weather would last all day.

Impey now asked for a chair to be brought out to him. He climbed onto the chair to enable to crowd to see and hear him more clearly. The action had an unfortunate result, with the section of the crowd who had previously been unruly deciding the Mayor's speech should not be heard this time. As he began to read the proclamation again the shouting, booing and abuse became so noisy that it was clear he could not be heard. Impey could not compete with the noise and gave up. He stepped down from the chair and the procession moved off again.

As they made their way towards the Town Hall, the Mayor and Civic party were subjected to more verbal abuse. Impey and Smith disappeared inside the building while a few of the Councillors remained on the steps to watch the rest of the procession before they went inside and the doors were closed. As the schoolchildren and the end of the procession made their way down Manchester Street the crowd surged forward milling around in front of the Town Hall.

Chief Constable Griffin had his policemen on duty at various points along the route and also a number who accompanied the procession. On duty outside the Town Hall, wearing their famous straw helmets, were four officers. Sergeants Frederick Smith and John Matsell were both veterans of the Luton Borough police, Smith being the force's senior sergeant wi:h over twenty-five years' service. The other two officers, Constables Albert Higgins and Charles Clements were both new recruits. Concerned with the hostility that a section of the crowd were showing and the tension that was building, the four policemen took up a position on the Town Hall steps as soon as the doors had closed behind the Civic party.

The crowd thronged around the front of the Town Hall and along George Street. A small group of men at the front were particularly vociferous. John Good and Sidney Quince, both of whom were well known to Sergeants Smith and Matsell, led the cries from the crowd to fetch out the Mayor and Town Clerk. Another man in the group, George Goodship, was also inciting the crowd, urging them to burst down the doors. He had already been told to keep quiet by Sergeant Smith who had seen him shouting and booing Impey while he was speaking. It was Goodship, Good and Quince, who led a group of men in a rush up the Town Hall steps, only to be forced back down by the police officers.

For the next ten minutes or so the four policemen held their

Peace Day 19th July 1919. 'Peace Enthroned, the Council's official float is behind the VAD nurses from Wardown. The procession has halted on Market Hill while the Mayor addresses the Ex-servicemen at the Town Hall. The photograph gives an excellent impression of the numerous crowds that lined the route.

Source: Luton Museum Service

position against mounting hostility and further attempts to rush them. They endeavoured to calm the crowd but the numerous cries to 'get Impey and Smith' were becoming more abusive and obscene. The situation grew more tense by the minute and was not helped by a potentially serious incident that was beginning to develop outside the Carnegie Library.

Constable Albert Sear had been on duty in George Street and began to make his way through the crowd to assist his colleagues at the Town Hall. Sear, another constable who was on duty for the first time, found himself being jostled and abused by a group of men. The weight of the crowd was gradually forcing him past the library towards Manchester Street and totally isolating him from the other police officers.

Realising Sear could be in some danger with the hostility that was developing, Sergeant Matsell together with Constable Higgins made their way from the Town Hall steps through the crowd to assist Sear. They reached him just in time, as he was being manhandled by people in the crowd. Sear had served with the 1st/5th Bedford's and Matsell, speaking to the mob who had surrounded the officers, demanded to know why they wanted to assault a man who had served alongside other Lutonians during the war. There was some abuse but Matsell was well known to many of the men and he defused the confrontation. The three policemen then began to make their way back to the Town Hall.

The temporary absence of the two officers at the Town Hall had put extra pressure on Sergeant Smith and Constable Clements and they had been forced back up the steps and against the doors. Overwhelmed by sheer weight of numbers the pressure finally told. With the men at the front linking arms, the two policemen were rushed again and the doors finally burst open. Sergeant Smith was bowled over and trampled on and Constable Clements was carried through the entrance into the vestibule. Among the first through were Goodship and Quince. It was just after 3.15pm.

As Mayor Impey and the Civic party returned into the Town Hall, Frederick Rignall watched the crowd from the doorway for a couple of minutes before closing the doors. An ex-policeman on the Luton Borough force, Rignall had left in June 1907 after being appointed manager of the Town Hall. The position also required him to carry out the duties of Sergeant at Arms to the Mayor as well as town Macebearer on civic occasions.

Inside the Town Hall, Impey, together with his wife, the Town Clerk

This print from the 'Luton News' is the only photograph to show the Civic party on Peace Day. (Unfortunately the negative has been destroyed) Mayor Impey can be seen standing on a chair reading the King's pryclarnation. To his left are William Smith, the Town Clerk, who is partly obscured by Frederick Rignafl, m top hat, the Mayor's Sergeant at Arns and Macebearer. Luton News Source: Luton Museum Service

and other guests, had retired to the Mayor's parlour. Other Councillors began getting ready to make their way to Wardown Park with their families who had watched the procession from the assembly room. Rignall made his way upstairs to his office next to the assembly room where his wife and four children were waiting. They watched as the crowd outside became more vociferous and hostile. Rignall, realising the mood of the crowd was becoming rather violent, made his way back downstairs to the Mayor's parlour to inform Impey and Smith of the growing tension. Deciding to get his family out of the Town Hall by means of the rear entrance, Rignall made his way across the vestibule to the foot of the staircase just at the moment the doors burst open and the mob spilled into the building.

The Peace Day Procession Route July 19th 1919

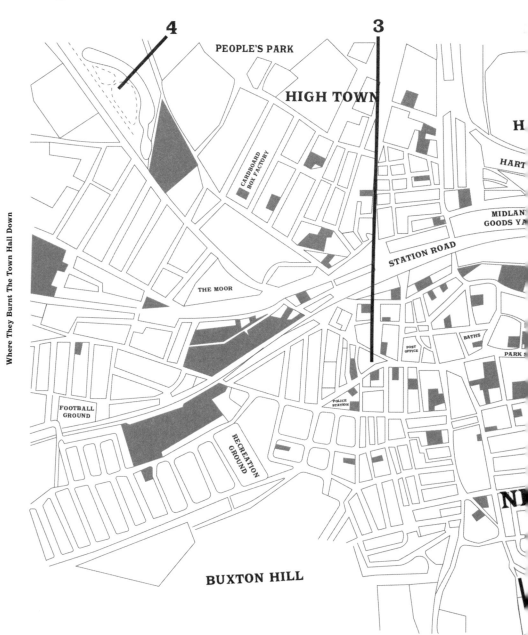

4

3

PEOPLE'S PARK

HIGH TOWN

H

HART

MIDLAN
GOODS YA

CARDBOARD
BOX FACTORY

STATION ROAD

Where They Burnt The Town Hall Down

THE MOOR

BATHS

PARK S

POST
OFFICE

POLICE
STATION

FOOTBALL
GROUND

RECREATION
GROUND

N

BUXTON HILL

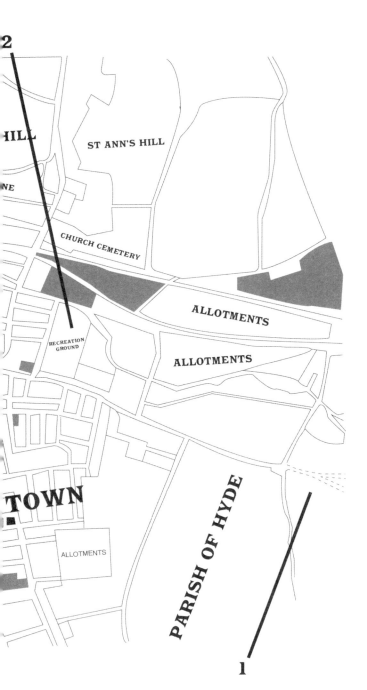

1: Luton Hoo Park

2: East Ward
Recreation
Ground

3: The Town Hall

4: Wardown Park

5: "Whitecroft"
Home of Mayor
Henry impey

Luton Town
Centre
July 1919

Where They Burnt The Town Hall Down

PRINCIPAL BUILDINGS

1. Police station & courthouse.

2. W.S. Clark
   S. Farmer & co
   Dillingham & son.

3. Town hall.

4. J. N. Brown & Co.

5. Carnegie library.

6. Caspars.

7. Herts motors.

8. Post office.

9. Corn exchange.

10. Ivy leaf club.

11. Fire station.

PRINCIPAL STREETS

A. Dunstable place

B. Stuart st.

C. Upper george st.

D. Gordon st.

E. Wellington st.

F. Manchester st.

G. Williamson st.

H. Bute st.

I. George st.

J. Chapel st.

K. Market hill.

L. Park st.

M. Church st.

Where They Burnt The Town Hall Down

One of the best photographs that survive of Peace Day. Police Sergeant John Matsell (centre rear) and PC Higgins (centre front) can be seen coming to the aid of PC Sear (centre left) outside the Carnegie library. All three policemen are wearing their straw helmets. An idea can be gained of how densely packed the crowd was. It is also interesting to look at the men in the photograph. Most are wearing straw boaters and there are a few servicemen. Surrounding the policemen however are a number of men in caps gesticulating at the officers. The man to the front right of PC Higgins, not wearing a hat, is Albert Smith who would later take part in the evening riot. Luton News/Source: Luton Museum Serivce

Rignall immediately ran back up the staircase through the assembly room to his office followed by a mob of around eighty men and some women. The leaders of the mob, seeing Rignall in his ceremonial clothes and believing he would lead them to the Mayor, demanded he let them into his office. Trying to explain that only his wife and children were inside, Rignall attempted to close the door. His action only succeeded in angering the mob further and they forced the door open, knocking Rignall over in the process. Finding that Impey was not in the office the mob made their way back into the assembly room.

Rignall took this opportunity to take his family downstairs and got them out of the Town Hall through the rear entrance. He then made his way back to the assembly room to find the mob venting its anger on anything they could lay their hands on. Tables, chairs and some crockery were still laid out from a function held the previous evening. The tables were overturned, chairs were thrown about the room and crockery together with wall mirrors were smashed. Light fittings were ripped off walls and a grand piano was also overturned and smashed. Unfortunately there were still some Councillors' wives in the room and they watched in terror at the systematic vandalising of the assembly room.

The casement doors were opened and a few men made their way outside onto the balcony and proceeded to pull down the electric illuminations and frame and tear down the flags and decorations that hung from the building. A few individuals took it upon themselves to start throwing some of the chairs from the assembly room over the balcony where they crashed to the pavement below.

Rignall had by now returned to the assembly room to find Sergeant Matsell and the other policemen powerless to prevent the wanton vandalism. Both Rignall and Matsell appealed to the mob to stop

19th July 1919: 3.00pm. The procession has passed through on its way to Wardown Park and the huge crowd in George Street has swarmed in front of the Town Hall. It is just before the rush into the building and the police officers can just be seen on the steps. The sign for Herts Motors, where petrol would later in the evening be stolen to fuel the fire, is on the right of the photograph. Source: Luton Museum Service

throwing out any more furniture as there were women and children outside and a very real chance that someone could be seriously injured, or even killed. John Stanley Long, who appeared to act as one of the leaders, rushed up to Rignall. Long had a string of convictions and was well known to the former policeman. He told Rignall not to interfere otherwise he would be next over the balcony. Long's demeanour was aggressive and his language obscene but others intervened and reminded Long that their intention was to find the Mayor, not to pick individual quarrels. Renewing their search, the mob made their way back down the staircase, smashing lampshades as they went, followed by the police officers and Rignall.

At Wardown Park, Chief Constable Griffin was in the process of concluding an orderly dispersal of the Peace procession participants when he received news of the trouble at the Town Hall. Griffin immediately gave orders to his second-in-command Inspector Frederick Janes to take some officers and return to the Town Hall by car. He also instructed Deputy Special Chief Constable Charles Robinson and his twenty special constables, who had taken part in the procession, to make their way back. Griffin himself set off on horseback accompanied by the other mounted policemen.

As he approached the Town Hall from Manchester Street Griffin could see the magnitude of the crowd that thronged George Street all the way along to the Corn Exchange. He estimated there were between eight and ten thousand people. The mounted officers together with Inspector Janes' car arrived together and they slowly made their way through the crowd into the building. They encountered the mob swarming round the Council chamber and other offices, smashing light fittings in their frustration at not finding the Mayor. The timing of Griffin's arrival could not have been better as attempts were being made to force the door of the Mayor's parlour. Prudently, the group inside had locked and barricaded the door after Rignall's earlier warning.

Griffin and Janes were immediately confronted by the leaders of the mob who demanded the right to see the Mayor. A heated discussion took place with the Chief Constable advising that nothing would happen until the Town Hall had been cleared of people. With the arrival of the special constables the police were able to escort the mob from the building. They then set to work removing the debris that littered the pavement taking it back inside the Town Hall before closing and bolting the doors. Griffin then posted his officers, mounted men and specials around the front of the Town Hall.

With calm restored Impey, his wife, William Smith and the other guests emerged from the Mayor's parlour. Chief Constable Griffin and the Town Clerk took stock of the damage in the Town Hall. The assembly room had been totally wrecked and a number of other offices had been vandalised. (It emerged later that the doors had only been bolted at the bottom. One of the bolts was faulty and had torn away from its bracket with the pressure on it.)

Outside, the mounted police officers had managed to ease the crowd back from the steps. Their attention was caught by a man in naval uniform who climbed the tramway standard in front of the Town Hall. Urged on by the crowd's cheers, he pulled down the four lines of flags that hung from the standard.

Attempts were also made to pull down the decorations from the building. One man, Ephraim Gore, came out of the crowd, lit a match and set light to some of the flags that were hanging down. Police Sergeant Parsons, rushed forward, pulled the flags down and extinguished the fire with his boots.

The vast majority of the crowd were good-humoured and orderly and they now watched a succession of men make their way to the steps of the Town Hall and make speeches. Gore was one of those who made his way forward. A long criminal record meant that he was well known to many of the longer serving police officers who now watched. The main thrust of his speech was dissatisfaction at the pension he was receiving having been discharged from the army in 1916.

Ernest Kempson came forward and directed his comments towards the police. He urged the crowd to get the Mayor out, the police he said were only capable of catching poachers. He berated one officer, Inspector Herbert Hunt, who he said had hidden behind a desk job rather than serve in the army. It was no surprise that Kempson was also well known to the police.

The crowd became very excited during a speech given by John Pursey who stood on the parapet of the steps and deliberately knocked off one of the lamps. He told the crowd to give the Mayor and Town Clerk five minutes and then they would go 'over the top' and have them out. Pursey then began a countdown of the minutes and then urged people to go in. A number of the crowd began to move forward but did not attempt to break through the police.

Inside the Town Hall Impey conferred with Griffin and Smith as to whether or not he should go out and address the crowd. The Town

Clerk felt that it would be an ill-advised move and the Chief Constable was not sure he could guarantee the Mayor's safety.

The afternoon events now took a different turn. About 4.00pm it became clear that Impey was not going to make an appearance. Some of the crowd were now doubting that he was even in the Town Hall. Pursey told the crowd that Impey was not inside and asked them to go with him to the Mayor's house. Another man now came forward.

Harry Miles, who only months earlier had been presented with the Military Medal by Mayor Impey, repeatedly said that he was a Bolshevist and a revolutionary and that if the crowd wanted him to, he would lead them to Impey's house. Inspector Janes told him to stop encouraging people, to which Miles asked if Janes was going to read the Riot Act. Eventually, Miles, together with Pursey and Kempson made their way along George Street towards London Road where Impey had his home, Whitecrofe, accompanied by over five hundred men, women and children.

With the possibility of further trouble breaking out at the Mayor's home, Griffin together with Inspector Janes and a number of police officers also made their way to London Road while the mounted police escorted the crowd. Griffin and his men arrived first at the Mayor's home and he deployed his officers outside the house and gardens.

The crowd arrived in a very excited and vocal mood and called for Impey to come out and talk to them. One or two tried to climb over the garden railings but were kept out by the police. Griffin asked for the crowd to disperse as the Mayor was not at home. Not satisfied with the Chief Constable's answer a number of the leaders started getting excited, and a number were shouting at him at the same time. Ernest Kempson was again prominent and in a raised voice said that no one should believe what the police said. If he could lie like them he would have a job on the force. Griffin told them to calm down and offered to take a spokesman with him into the house to prove that the Mayor was not there. His proposal was accepted and after a quick discussion a spokesman was nominated. Griffin took him into the house and after a few minutes both emerged with the crowd's spokesman making it clear to them that no one was at home. The crowd voiced some noisy disappointment but slowly they began to make their way back to the town centre with the police not far behind.

The situation at the Town Hall remained relatively calm for the next hour. Indeed many people appeared to think that what had so far occurred was nothing more than rather boisterous antics caused by a small rowdy group and the majority of the crowd remained good-natured. It was not raining quite so heavily now and many people had decided to make their way to Wardown Park. Even so a crowd of some four thousand people remained in George Street.

Grievances continued to be aired from the Town Hall steps by various speakers and each was greeted with cheers and applause. The police attitude towards the speakers had relaxed somewhat but around 5.30pm they were called into action to prevent another break-in.

A number of men made their way towards the steps and made repeated attempts to get past the police line. Inspector Hunt recognised one of the men, Albert Smith, as he pushed him back. Smith was conspicuous as he was wearing a union flag around his neck. Earlier in the afternoon, he had been involved in the incident with Constable Sear. The threat came to nothing but shortly afterwards Smith again made his way to the steps and proceeded to count down the few minutes that remained until 6.00pm. As the Town Hall clock struck the hour he announced that he was now off for some beer but would be back to go 'over the top'. Together with Smith a large number of people made their way to the town's public houses; it was opening time.

Chief Constable Griffin was however still concerned with the size of the crowd that remained. He and the Town Clerk now made a series of phone calls. Griffin contacted neighbouring police forces advising them of the events that had taken place and requesting support. None was available locally and so he tried London, again without success. Peace celebrations were stretching police manpower to the limit.

William Smith meanwhile had conversations with Mr W. Clay, president of the DS&S and Mr W. Mair asking them if they would come to the Town Hall. Mair had been prominent in the food strike in 1918 but had subsequently become the first Labour magistrate in the town. Both men agreed and arrived just before 6.30pm and Griffin and Smith asked them if they would both speak to the crowd in an attempt to persuade them to disperse. They were both happy to do so but Clay made it very clear that in no way was he admitting to any involvement by DS&S members by consenting to address the crowd.

Clay and Mair, accompanied by Griffin and Smith came out onto the Town Hall steps. With their appearance the crowd quietened down and listened attentively to what both men had to say.

They disassociated themselves from the demonstrations and condemned what had occurred. Clay received a tremendous ovation from the crowd when speaking on behalf of the Federation and 'our noble dead' he appealed for order and for people to stop causing any further trouble or damage. They were, he continued only destroying their own property and putting the lives of women and children in danger. The best thing they could do now was to make their way to Wardown Park and enjoy the celebrations that were still taking place there. Clay and Mair were warmly received and their appearance had some effect with large numbers of people gradually making their way down Manchester Street towards the park.

Between one and two thousand people remained in George Street and Griffin now felt he was able to send a number of his officers back to the police station in Dunstable Place.

At Wardown Park the sports and entertainments had taken place throughout the afternoon with many people totally unaware of the events that had occurred at the Town Hall. Although the rain had dampened a lot of the enthusiasm, crowds in the park numbered almost twenty thousand people.

As the evening wore on, attention shifted to Popes Meadow and the fireworks display that had been organised. When the scheduled start time of 9.30pm came and went without anything happening people began to get restless. A number of groups started their own displays even though they had been requested not to. Eventually the fireworks display got under way but turned out to be rather disappointing in the wet conditions. By now news of the afternoon's trouble had filtered through to most people and in large numbers they began to make their way back to the town centre. There was a strong sense of anticipation that further events were about to unfold at the Town Hall.

The size of the crowd in front of the Town Hall began to increase substantially and quickly doubled to around four thousand stretching back to Bute Street. Inside the Town Hall, Chief Constable Griffin became concerned at the ever increasing numbers. The Mayor and his wife were still in the building together with the Town Clerk, Aldermen Arnold and Oakley, Councillors Barford and Escott and Mrs Escott. Frederick Rignall was also still there. He had by now changed back into civilian clothes and Griffin asked if he would go outside and mingle with the crowd to ascertain their mood. Rignall slipped out through the rear entrance into Upper George Street but returned within a few minutes. What he had seen and heard was not good news for Griffin.

Although the general mood of the crowd was good-natured there were a number of groups that had formed of a distinctly troublesome nature. Drink had also had its effect on some in the crowd and Rignall

19th July 1919: 4.10pm. The crowd in front of the Town Hall has thinned out with the departure of a large number to the Mayor's house in London Road. Decorations and flags have been pulled down after the rush into the building. (Compare with the previous photograph taken at 3.00pm.) Source: Luton Museum Service

Where They Burnt The Town Hall Down

also heard new words being sung to a popular war tune, 'The Old Barbed Wire'. 'If you want to find old Impey, I know where he is, I know where he is, He's hanging on the old Town Hall, I've seen him, I've seen him'. Griffin decided that the Mayor and the rest of the civic party should leave the building immediately.

The Mayoress and Mrs Escott were the first to be escorted from the rear entrance. Mrs Impey was in such a state of distress by this time that she was continually bursting into tears when anyone spoke to her. Next it was the turn of the Mayor and it was generally agreed that it would be better if he left in some form of disguise. After some quick discussion it was decided that he should put on the uniform of a special constable. In this ignominious way Henry Impey, Mayor of Luton, left his official residence for the last time and made his way to the Corporation Workhouse in Dunstable Road. He was followed by Messrs Arnold, Oakley, Barford and Escott. It was just before 10.00pm.

Chief Constable Griffin remained in the Town Hall together with William Smith and Fred Rignall. Griffin's resources were limited. He had available fifty-two regular policemen, four of whom were on duty at Popes Meadow, and this included his four mounted officers. He also had forty special constables including one mounted man.

He deployed officers in front of the Town Hall, in Upper George Street and Manchester Street with a few inside the building. Inspector

The time this photograph was taken is not clear and it is unfortunate that the area around the Town Hall entrance is blurred. The number of people on the steps however leads me to believe it was probably taken at about 6.30pm when Messrs. Clay, the DS&S President, and Mair were addressing the crowd. Source: Luton Museum Serivce

Herbert Hunt was placed in command on the Upper George Street side and Inspector Frederick Janes on the Manchester Street side. Griffin remained in overall control. He left around a third of his force in reserve at the police station.

The mood of the crowd now took a distinct turn for the worse. A large and unruly element had come into the town and made their way to the Town Hall just after 10.00pm. On the way they had armed themselves with stones, bricks, iron bars and some bottles. It was also clear that many of them had spent the evening in the public bars. If anyone was in doubt that there would be any more trouble it seemed the question had been answered.

Whether or not it was a pre-arranged signal, trouble broke out as the peace 'flares' were lit on the hills around the town and illuminated the town centre. A hail of missiles rained down on the Town Hall and within a short time nearly all of the windows in the building were broken. It was clear that the mood of the evening was going to be in sharp contrast to what had taken place in the afternoon. A sudden rush was then made by a large body of men at the police line in front of the Town Hall. As the officers were confronted, the mob were urged on by shouts and cries from the crowd.

George Heley was particularly noticeable in his naval uniform. An able seaman serving aboard HMS Violent, he had earlier taken part in the procession as part of the Jack Cornwell tableau. Heley now seemed intent on taking on the police force single-handed. He hit Constable Ellingham on the jaw and Constable Gardner in the stomach before kicking Constable Simpkins in a rather tender area!

George Fowler, who had earlier been at the Mayor's home, was among a group of men who reached the Town Hall steps. As Constable Wood tried to stop him, he pulled the officer to the ground and kicked him in the back. Inspector Hunt while assisting another injured constable was knocked off his feet by the rush but recovered sufficiently to lead his men in clearing the steps and driving the mob back from the entrance. The doors of the Town Hall had held, helped to some extent by the fact that they had been barricaded with tables earlier in the evening.

With the police effort concentrated on the front a few men took advantage of gaining access into the Town Hall through the windows of the Food Office at the front on the Manchester Street side of the building. Using piles of ration books and coupons they proceeded to start fires. Inspector Janes and his men were kept busy ejecting intruders using their truncheons when necessary. While trying to prevent a man starting a fire in the Town Clerk's Office, Fred Rignall was hit by a missile and knocked over but was not seriously hurt. The fires in the Food Office however were starting to take hold and at 10.25pm Griffin put through a telephone call to the Fire Brigade.

Luton Fire Station was situated at the corner of Church Street and St. Mary's Road, not more than a quarter mile away from the Town Hall. In charge of the Fire Brigade was Chief Officer Alexander Andrew. When Andrew received the call from the Chief Constable he had five men on duty for the evening. The day had been quiet with the brigade attending only two small fires in Bailey Street and Salisbury Road during the evening. Griffin had reported small fires in the Town Hall and realising that the town centre was full of people, Andrew decided that the building's internal hydrant should be sufficient to extinguish the fires. He therefore sent his second officer, Jesse Plummer, on foot, together with three other firemen, in answer to the call. Plummer was an ideal choice. He was a volunteer fireman and during the day worked for Rignall at the Town Hall. The firemen arrived at the building, got the hydrant at the rear of the assembly room into action and with the help of Fred Rignall, set about putting out the fires.

Outside the Town Hall missiles continued to be thrown at the police and the windows, other attempts were made to rush the front entrance without success and there were numerous minor casualties on both sides.

Griffin now made the decision to go on the offensive to try to clear the crowds away from the Town Hall and hopefully disperse them from George Street. All his officers, both regular and specials, were now on duty in the vicinity of the building. Griffin gave the order for a number of his men to make a baton charge. Forming in extended line in Upper George Street, the policemen drew their truncheons, ran down the street past the Town Hall and charged into the crowd. The police struck out at anyone who was in their way and initially they drove the crowd back as far as Wellington Street but with George Street so densely packed, the momentum of the charge broke up on a wall of people.

Inevitably violent clashes broke out. Constable Riches was struck a blow over the left eye with a stick wielded by William Dixon but in turn knocked Dixon to the ground. As he urged the crowd to resist the police, Charles Lambert was also struck by a police truncheon but not before he had punched Constable Higham in the face. Missiles were also being thrown at the policemen and taking a toll and those who were badly injured were helped back into the Town Hall.

Inspector Hunt was again in the thick of the action and received a heavy blow to the head. Colleagues assisted him back into the building but his condition was considered so serious that he was taken immediately to the nearby Bute hospital by police ambulance and Inspector Duncombe took over.

The Luton Fire Brigade circa. 1918. Seated centre is Chief Officer Alexander Andrew. The photograph as probably taken at the time of the delivery of the brigade's second motor fire engine.
W. H. Cox/ Source: Luton Museum Service

The police had by now suffered a number of casualties and they were being attended to by the Luton medical officer of health and police surgeon, Dr William Archibald. He had arrived at the Town Hall at 11.00pm and had utilised the Council chamber as a treatment room. The injuries were mainly minor cuts and abrasions but a few officers were being treated for more serious head injuries.

Although the charge had not had the desired effect, Griffin decided on another baton charge, this time on the Manchester Street side, where attempts were being made to force a side door of the Town Hall. In the melee, Constable Roberts was attacked by George Fowler, who had earlier injured Constable Wood. Fowler was aiming blows at Roberts with a large stick but the officer managed to hit him a hard blow with his truncheon which felled Fowler.

Meanwhile other officers were engaged in several charges in front of the Town Hall as they struggled with sections of the crowd. During one of these Sergeant Parsons was separated from other officers and confronted by a number of men. Among them was George Bodsworth who, attempting to hit Parsons, was struck first. Others grabbed the Sergeant and as colleagues came to his aid a 'tug of war' developed before the mob were driven off. Bodsworth meanwhile had turned his attention elsewhere, hitting Constable Stanbridge in the general mayhem that was taking place.

Many people were inciting the gangs to attack the police. Noticeable among them was Maud Kitchener. Dressed in army tunic and cap she was using violent and abusive language and continually urging anybody to attack the police. There was no love lost between Maud and the officers many of whom had arrested her on numerous occasions in the past.

In a final effort to try and break up the crowd, Chief Constable Griffin included his mounted officers in a charge. Unfortunately some men had got hold of a couple of hand carts and these were pushed in front of the advancing horses. As Special Constable Gilham reigned his horse in, it was so brutally stabbed that it had to be destroyed two days later.

Once again the charge failed to make any impression. Griffin's decision to go on the offensive had not worked and many of his officers had been injured. It had only fuelled the anger of many people who were now intent on further destruction before the night was out.

In the Town Hall Jesse Plummer and his firemen had succeeded in controlling the original fire in the Food Office but as quickly as one blaze was put out another would be started. With easy access through the Town Hall windows a number of men were becoming bolder and chancing their arm in the building and Inspector Janes and his men had their hands full clearing them out. Albert Smith who had been outside the Town Hall in the afternoon had now managed to get inside. With a friend, Stanley Dolby, he was lingering near one of the toilets. As he entered he was spotted by Inspector Janes who promptly followed him in, hit Smith with his truncheon and then threw him and Dolby out of the building. A number of men had gathered in a corridor behind the office of the Town Clerk but they were broken up and ejected when Janes and his officers charged them.

Missiles thrown through the windows had again taken their toll and all three of Plummer's men had been hit but at least they now had the situation under control. Then disaster struck the firemen; the internal hydrant failed and cut off the flow of water. With no supply available smouldering fires particularly in the Food Office began to flare up again. Plummer was left with no alternative but to phone Chief Officer Andrew and advise him that fires were still alight in the Town Hall. He and his injured men could do no more and would return to the fire station.

Andrew, driving the brigade's newer motor fire engine, together with firemen W. Burgess and J. Garrett, left the station at 11.07pm. Arriving in Manchester Street by way of Guildford Street and Williamson Street he parked the engine and the firemen quickly assessed that they could easily contain the fire using the engine's first aid apparatus. This consisted of an auxiliary pump and small reel of hose which could be brought into action in a few seconds. The firemen were getting the apparatus ready when a group broke away from the crowd and rushed them. Both Burgess and Garrett were hit and could not help Andrew who was prevented from fighting the fire by the mob. The fire engine was surrounded and three men clambered onto it. One of them Frederick Plater was distinctively dressed in clerical clothes.

Dispensing with the hose, Andrew was forced to defend himself and took the extreme measure of drawing his fire axe, telling the men that if they did not get off the engine he would be forced to use it, and he would not use the flat end! His action worked and the Chief Officer, realising that any further attempt to put out the blaze was useless, started the fire engine and slowly reversed it. Stones began to be thrown as he moved away and the mob rushed the vehicle again, causing damage to the front lamps and horn but Andrew put the vehicle into forward gear and forced the fire engine through the crowd and away from the scene. Although still faced with a hail of missiles from the hostile crowd the firemen's brass helmets gave them some measure of protection and they returned safely to the station. Behind them at the Town Hall the fire in the Food Office was beginning to take hold.

The situation had now become a full scale riot with a level of violence that nobody could have predicted. It was one thing to confront charging police officers but assaulting firemen, preventing them doing their job was another matter altogether. The crowd were in a mood of triumphant control and those policemen who were not injured were reduced to ejecting the numerous intruders from the Town Hall. William Dixon, who minutes earlier had hit Constable Riches during a baton charge, was confronted by Deputy Special Constable Robinson who knocked him to the floor. As Dixon attempted to get away he was struck again by another constable. Outside, Constable Sear, who had been involved in the afternoon fracas, was knocked unconscious when he was hit by a brick and he joined Inspector Hunt in Bute Hospital.

The rioters now realised that with the police powerless to intervene they could do as they pleased. The glass-panelled doors of Herts Motors

From
Looton.

To Commemorate

"Town Hall" Goes West.

'19.

I.L.I.S

Ltd in George Street were smashed in and a man emerged carrying two gallon cans of petrol. Making his way to the Town Hall he was able to empty the contents onto the fires in the Food Office. Broken window frames and burning boxes were also hurled into the building to help fuel the blaze. Shortly after, the chemist shop of W. S. Clark, on the corner of Wellington Street and George Street, had its windows broken. Bottles of perfume became the target for looters but most of its stock of bottles was used as ammunition and thrown into the burning Town Hall. The building was by now well alight on the Manchester Street side and the internal walls, mostly constructed of wood, were beginning to catch alight. The main structure was still largely unaffected but the decision was made to evacuate the police casualties to the police station

At the fire station Chief Officer Andrew now put into operation another plan in an attempt to get to the Town Hall and fight the blaze. After phoning to arrange for police help he sent five men led by his foreman T. George carrying hoses and equipment, to make their way by foot to Dunstable Place. From there, under the protection of police and special constables led by Inspector Duncombe, they could connect to hydrants in Upper George Street. Shortly afterwards Andrew, again driving the new engine with two men on board, left the fire station. Driving without lights and taking a route that kept well away from the rioters he arrived in Dunstable Place unobserved and joined his other men. The firemen got one hose connected to a hydrant while police officers stood guard as they took the hose towards the Town Hall the rioters saw the firemen and immediately rushed toward them. Missiles were thrown and a length of hose was seized, its couplings being thrown at the firemen. Andrew had quickly connected another hose and it was now turned on the rioters to keep them at bay. With a further hose in action on the crowd the firemen were able to prevent the rioters getting near to them and a row of police officers gave as much protection as they could. Even so several attempts were made to cut the hoses. Missiles continued to be thrown at the firemen and one by one Andrews' men suffered injuries that forced them to seek medical treatment at the police station. Their places were taken by policemen who were assisted by a number of civilians and servicemen who had offered to help.

In the police station Dr Archibald was treating the injured in the parade room. There was such a constant stream of casualties that he requested the assistance of another doctor, F. Seymour Lloyd. Police officers, firemen and the occasional civilian were being patched up before returning to duty.

The Town Hall clock had struck midnight to accompanying cheers from the crowd and slowly the fire had taken a complete hold of the building. The policemen evacuated the building about 12.30pm. Griffin, Smith and Rignall, who had stayed as long as possible, now made their way to the police station. Shortly afterwards the clock crashed down followed by the bell tower and gradually the roof. The flames from the blaze that now raged in the Town Hall illuminated the whole scene of destruction.

It was obvious to Chief Officer Andrew that the building was now beyond saving. All his firemen were now at the scene and two more hoses were operating from the top of Gordon Street and Dunstable Place. These were now being directed towards the adjoining buildings at the rear of the Town Hall to prevent the fire from spreading. The other hoses were still employed in keeping the rioters at bay.

Second Officer Plummer was directing the brigade's operations in Gordon Street. Andrew told him to take some men into Manchester Street where there were more hydrants to help prevent the fire spreading to the Salvation Army Barracks adjacent to the Town Hall. As the water was turned on and he took a hose nearer several men rushed Plummer. He was struck on the back of his head and then punched as he fell. His assailant was Frederick Plater still dressed in clerical clothes, who had earlier threatened Chief Officer Andrew. Plummer was helped to a house in Manchester Street where he received some medical assistance from the wife of the tenant before returning to duty.

By 1.00am the confrontation had reached stalemate. The two sides held their ground, the authorities the area to the west of the Town Hall, the crowd to the east along George Street.

For the fourth time during the day, Albert Smith was prominent in the proceedings. Together with Frederick Couldridge he was throwing bottles and stones at the firemen in Upper George Street.

Where They Burnt The Town Hall Down

In an attempt to get nearer Smith crept along the pavement but he was spotted by the firemen who turned their hose on him. The force of the water jet knocked Smith off his feet. Undaunted, he managed to get to Dillingham's hat warehouse shortly after and proceeded to throw a number of cartons into the street. Stripping to the waist, Smith picked one of the cartons up and began beating it like a drum, urging the crowd on.

The missile throwing continued, although it had by this time become more sporadic. Three hours had passed since the trouble had begun and the enthusiasm of many in the crowd was slowly beginning to evaporate. The sound of shattering glass lifted their spirits once again.

The windows of J. N. Brown and Co., a boot and shoe shop in Manchester Street were smashed and once again it was Frederick Plater who was involved, breaking them with a stick. He removed some boots and other items from the display and handed them on to people nearby. Other looters quickly made off with much of the stock as it was passed among the crowd.

It was however the music shop and warehouse of S. Farmer and Co. that now provided the rioters and the crowd with their next source of evening entertainment.

The plate glass windows of the ground floor showroom were shattered and looters made off with a number of gramophones. Rioters then dragged out a piano and a pianola which were taken to Wellington Street and Bute Street. Another grand piano was pulled out onto the pavement in front of the showroom and it was not long before the crowd had found a pianist.

It was a surreal scene that now met the eye. Against the backdrop of the blazing Town Hall and the tumult of the rioters and crowd, could be heard the strains of 'Keep the home fires burning' coming from the solitary piano. People were quick to join in, giving a rousing rendition and then carrying on with other popular wartime songs. A couple climbed onto the piano and began dancing and soon others in the street were joining in. The riot seemed to have intoxicated everyone.

The singing and dancing carried on, accompanied by sporadic outbursts of missile throwing. The fire brigade continued to use their hoses in keeping the rioters at bay as well as trying to contain the fire. Just before 2.00am Chief Officer Andrew ordered the fire engine, parked in Dunstable Place, to be driven back to the station to prevent the rioters from causing any further damage to it.

Chief Constable Griffin had made further requests for police reinforcements throughout the evening to no avail. Realising the only hope of quelling the riot was to demand help from the military, he had contacted the War Office. Still no help was forthcoming and so the decision was made by Griffin and William Smith to telephone Cecil Harmsworth, the town's MP who was in London. Harmsworth told Smith he would go straight to the War Office to demand action.

Harmsworth was as good as his word, for within the hour permission was given to allow troops to come to the aid of Griffin. Just before 3.00am an advance guard of men from the Royal Field Artillery stationed at Biscot Camp, less than a mile north of the Town Hall, marched down Upper George Street from Dunstable Road to be followed shortly after by a larger body of troops. Following quick consultation between Griffin and their commanding officer the soldiers, eight abreast and singing, marched down to the Town Hall and formed a cordon around the building. Their arrival was greeted with cheering from the crowd and immediately hundreds of people began to leave the town centre. It was clear nobody wanted any confrontation with the military authorities.

It was to be some time however before George Street was completely clear. Further damage to property was caused in Bute Street as people made their way home. The hairdressing salon of Mr Carl Caspers had its windows broken and a stock of umbrellas stolen. The fact that Caspers was a German national was clearly the reason his premises were attacked even though he was married to an English woman and had commenced his business in Luton in 1892. The shop windows of Mr H. Stern were also damaged.

Griffin contemplated calling out a magistrate to read the Riot Act but at this stage of the night it was decided that there was now very little point.

With the arrival of the military, Chief Officer Andrew was now able to concentrate his brigade's attention on putting out the fire in the Town Hall for the first time since the riot had begun. Both fire engines returned to the scene and his brigade now directed all their efforts on the building. By 4.30am the firemen had virtually extinguished the blaze. At 5.00am Griffin was able to dismiss the special constables from duty.

With daylight the extent of the damage to the Town Hall could be seen for the first time. The building had been completely gutted except for the ground floor offices on Upper George Street used by the education department. The firemen remained busy damping down smouldering material and pulling down internal walls that were in a dangerous state.

About 9.00am the entire locality around the Town Hall came under military control. A body of Royal Engineers arrived from Bedford to relieve the R.F.A. troops. They threw a cordon round the building and placed guard details on street corners and at all the premises that had been vandalised. The full fury of the night's rioting had at last been recognised by the authorities. The Royal Engineers wore full active service kit including steel helmets and each carried fifty rounds of ammunition.

Police reinforcements also arrived during the morning from several local forces which boosted Chief Constable Griffin's manpower to around two hundred men and his own officers were able to be released from duty.

20th July 1919: 1.00am. The Town Hall is well alight and by this time the clock and bell tower together with the roof had collapsed into the building.

Source: Luton Museum Service

Where They Burnt The Town Hall Down

The rain that had fallen for most of the previous twenty-four hours now came down even harder. The weather though did not prevent hordes of men, women and children coming to George Street throughout the day to view the result of the riot. The Drumhead Memorial service due to be held at Luton Hoo in the afternoon was cancelled; the inclement weather was given as the reason, but it was unthinkable that the service could go ahead anyway.

During Sunday afternoon the crowd of onlookers increased so that from 6.30pm George Street was once again densely packed with people and it seemed that many were waiting in anticipation of further trouble breaking out. They were not to be disappointed.

By the evening control of the town had been handed back to Chief Constable Griffin and his police and the majority of the military had gone off duty, leaving only small detachments maintaining discreet guard patrol.

Shortly after 9.00pm in a carbon copy of the previous evening, noisy, rowdy elements infiltrated the main crowd. This time they congregated at the Corn Exchange. A window was smashed in one of the adjoining public toilets and calls were made to burn the Corn Exchange down. Some of the leaders believing that Lady Wernher was still the owner of the property, convinced the mob they should turn their attention elsewhere as no one had any argument with her Ladyship.

The main post office in Cheapside was suggested as a possible target but it was thought that military guard patrols were in the vicinity. Others said that a sailor was being held in custody at the police station and they should go there and demand his release. There were enough of them to take on the police again if he was not set free and this idea aroused a lot of excitement among the crowd who considered this to be the best plan. They clearly had no idea that the police had been reinforced. Around a thousand people now made their way to Dunstable Place and gathered outside the police station. A group of younger men were acting as the leaders and they began inciting the crowd, making speeches and urging everyone to rush the police station and set the sailor free. One person who voiced agreement with these sentiments was Albert Smith.

Chief Constable Griffin came to the station gates and made an earnest appeal for order and no further trouble. He then advised the crowd to disperse and go home and many who were mere onlookers not wanting to get involved left but the majority remained and began behaving in a provocative manner. Griffin appealed to them again; enough trouble had been caused and he had no wish for further confrontation. Cries again began for the sailor to be brought out and released but the Chief Constable said that he was no longer in the station having returned to his depot. A menacing attitude was now developing in the crowd with many demanding that they should be allowed in to see for themselves.

Stones were then thrown at the gates and Griffin decided the time for talking was over. He had assembled his officers in the station yard with their truncheons drawn and as the gates were opened ordered them to charge. The mob scattered immediately they saw the number of policemen who came streaming out of the gates. Striking out at anyone who was in their way the police drove the mob out of Dunstable

Place into Stuart Street. Many people, both men and women, were knocked down in the charge. Maud Kitchener lay in the gutter less than fifty yards from the gates. The prospect of an ugly confrontation developed in Stuart Street as some men stopped and started to pull down some iron railings. For once good sense prevailed and the men decided to drop the railings and ran off.

The police charge carried on into Wellington Street and Upper George Street before they commenced a general clearance of George Street. Many people still refused to leave as they were chased from one street to another. In Adelaide Terrace, a stone just missed Sergeant Clark who then watched the man who had thrown it, Albert Smith, disappear into his house. A particularly rowdy gang of youths remained in the vicinity of the Plait Hall in Cheapside throwing missiles at the police. They had armed themselves with rubble from a road that was under repair. Griffin decided the only answer was a thorough sweep and clearance of all the streets between George Street and the railway and eventually the last gangs were chased across the railway footbridge up into High Town area and beyond the Corn Exchange into Park Street and off into New Town area.

It was not until midnight that calm was completely restored in the town but even so the police kept a watchful eye through the rest of the night. Dr Archibald treated one policeman from the Bedford force, (the charge had knocked him off his feet and he was trampled on by his colleagues), and one civilian for serious injuries. Doctors however found themselves busy on Monday morning and numerous bandaged heads were hidden under boaters or hats.

Monday was much quieter during the day with people back at work. The fire brigade were in attendance at the Town Hall again to help demolish the outer walls of the Food Office which were in danger of collapsing. They finally left the scene for the last time at 12.05pm.

The evening again saw large crowds begin to congregate in George Street and the police were out in force. They patrolled the area in groups of three and this avoided the possibility of an officer on duty on his own being attacked.

At about 11.00pm a large group of men once again began to behave in an aggressive manner near the Corn Exchange. For the third night running it appeared that a serious situation was about to develop. Within fifteen minutes a large body of police led by Chief Constable Griffin was marched from the police station and formed in extended order in front of the Town Hall. Griffin issued warnings to the crowd to make their way home otherwise the police would be forced to break them up and would treat anyone who remained on the streets in the same manner.

Most people took the Chief Constable's advice and left immediately but a small number of gangs remained in defiance of the police order. At 11.30pm Griffin ordered his officers to make a baton charge along George Street and the gangs were scattered in all directions. There were a couple of minor attempts at resistance, Stanley Dolby threw a large stone that hit Constable Coupar of the Herts force on the leg, before the police had control and then started a clean up along adjoining streets. They met little resistance apart from a confrontation in Chapel Street.

One gang remained particularly unruly. They pulled down a brick wall on the corner of New Street and Chapel Street, then made their way back to George Street and threw bricks at the police. The officers charged and as the gang turned and ran up Chapel Street they threw more bricks at windows causing damage to a dozen properties including Partridge's cycle shop. Another body of police arrived and charged the gang from Stuart Street, forcing them to scatter and disappear among the streets of New Town.

It had been the last act of defiance, the Peace Riots were over.

Next page: 20th July 1919: 5.00am. Firemen can be seen directing water into the food office of the Town Hall where the initial fires were started. Groups of soldiers from the Royal Field Artillery based at Biscot Camp mill around in George Street while the rain continues to fall. Source: Luton Museum Service

Where They Burnt The Town Hall Down

JOY DAY RIOT AT LUTON. TH
JULY 19TH-20TH 1919.

OWN HALL ON FIRE, 5.AM.

Where They Burnt The Town Hall Down

The Town Hall, Sunday 20th July. The rain was coming down even harder but it does not stop Lutonians coming to look at the ruins throughout the day.
Source: Luton Central Library

View looking into the main budding of the Town Hall. Remains of the roof can be seen through the ground floor window.
Source: Luton Central Library

Monday 21st July. The fire brigade are still in attendance preparing to demolish the outer walls of the Food Office on the right of the building.
Luton News/Source: Luton Museum Service

Workmen can be seen making the Town Hall ruin safe. Very few people take any interest. The rain has stopped and the sun is shining. The riots are over.
Source: Luton Museum Service

Where They Burnt The Town Hall Down

Monday 21st July.
The remains of the food office, which were in a dangerous state, can be seen in the process of being demolished.
W. H. Cox/Source: Luton Museum Service

The Aftermath July-October 1919

On the Sunday morning after the riot, the town's MP, Cecil Harmsworth, travelled from London to visit the scene with the Chief Constable. He was followed on the Monday by Sir Leonard Dunning, HM Inspector of Constabulary who fully endorsed the decision taken by Griffin and Smith in requesting military aid and police reinforcements.

During Monday a search was carried out in the Town Hall ruins to see if anything had survived the ravages of the fire. Very little had. The Town Clerk had put a number of documents into two safes during Peace Day afternoon. These were located and opened but all the contents had perished. The Mayor's robes were destroyed as was a store of food held in the cellar. The Mace was found but was in a badly damaged condition. (it would subsequently be renovated.) Numerous historical documents and pictures were lost forever.

On Monday night a call was put through to the fire brigade at 11.00pm to say that Wardown House was on fire. Chief Officer Andrew and his men responded immediately but were the victims of a hoax call. When they arrived at the park they found everything quiet and no sign of any fire.

The Town Council held three emergency meetings behind closed doors at the Courthouse in Stuart Street on the Sunday evening and on Monday morning and evening. In the absence of Mayor Impey, who had left Luton with his wife early on the Sunday morning, Alderman Arnold was elected to preside over the meetings. They met again as scheduled on the Tuesday evening and this time the meeting was opened to members of the press. A lengthy statement was delivered by Arnold in which he described the circumstances that had led to the refusal of the use of Wardown Park by the Council. Councillor Briggs stated that he wished to disassociate himself from the refusal as he had not taken part in reaching the decision.

The police and fire brigade were thanked for the action they had taken and some of the brigade's brass helmets covered in dents, bearing testimony to the violence of the riot, were shown to the Councillors.

Three letters that had been received during the day by the Town Clerk were then read out. The letters, from the Luton Labour Party, the DS&S and the Comrades, all condemned the rioting that had taken place and pledged their support for the Council and any measures they considered necessary to maintain peace. In their letter the DS&S emphasised that none of their members had any involvement in the riot.

As a result of the meeting a public notice issued by the Town Clerk 'To The Inhabitants' was published in the press and put on placards around the town. The notice contained a resume of the meeting and concluded *'They (the Council) are determined to uphold the law and preserve the King's Peace, and to govern the town in conformity with their powers. Stern measures will be adopted prevent, or overcome, any further symptoms of riot, and the inhabitants a-e advised and strongly urged not to congregate in the streets, either during the day or night, and to proceed with their business quietly and peaceably. The Council have the utmost faith that this request will be readi.'y complied with for the general benefit of the community'. The notice was issued 'By the unanimous Order of the Council'*

On the same day Lady Wernher contacted the DS&S with a view to rearranging the Drumhea6 memorial service. She felt the service should go ahead as quickly as possible and offered the use of Luton Hoo Park for the forthcoming Sunday, the 27th. Agreement was sought with Chief Constable Griffir who voiced no objection provided that no procession was held and the service was set for 2.00pm.

On Thursday 24th, Henry Impey paid a brief visit to the town arriving by train at around 12.30am. William Smith had kept Impey informed of developments by phone during the week. Impey met with Smith in the Catnegie library lecture hall which was serving as offices for the Town Clerk's department and they discussed the ongoing situation. He stayed for an hour but before departing gave local reporters an interview. Impey explained that after leaving the Town Hall he and his wife had stayed at the Union Workhouse before being driven to Harringay around 6.00am on the Sunday morning. He gave two reasons for his absence from the town. Both he and his wife were suffering from bad health. Impey had fainted four times during the Sunday and his wife had suffered a nervous breakdown, and both of them had hardly slept the previous five nights. Also the Chief Constable and Town Clerk had advised him to keep a low profile. His visit, he said, was brief because he wanted to be with his wife but when events had settled down he intended to return to Luton and continue as Mayor.

The Drumhead memorial service was duly held on the Sunday and in total contrast to the previous weekend the weather was warm and sunny. The DS&S had taken responsibility for making the arrangements and in an outbreak of unity were fully supported by the Comrades together with the Clergy of all denominations and several local bands. A site had been chosen in the park within easy reach of Park Street an estimated crowd of twenty thousand attended the service. Lady Wernher had arranged for a platform to be erected from which the clergy conducted the service. Dressed in black, Lady Wernher together with her son Major Harold Wernher stood in front of the platform and behind them were the ex-servicemen lined up with no regard to the organisation they belonged to. Among them were a number of disabled men who had been transported to the service in a charabanc provided by Lady Wernher. They included a veteran of the Crimean war of 1854/5.

After the service Lady Wernher met with Clay and Cooper of the

Boarded up shops n George Street after the riot. On the corner with Wellington Street is the chemi3t shop of W. S. Clark. Next to it is S. Farmer and Co from where the pianos were taken and to the far right, the hat factory of Dillingham and Sons.
Source: Luton Central Library

DS&S and two representatives from the Comrades. She offered them an invitation to the afternoon of sports and refreshments at Luton Hoo Park on Saturday 16th August which she had provisionally discussed with Mayor Impey a few weeks earlier. This was gratefully accepted and as Lady Wernher was driven away in her car she was given a rousing send off by the crowd.

The police had begun making enquiries as to the identity of rioters on the Sunday morning. The investigation was led by Detective Sergeant Arthur Bacon together with Detective Constable Horace Frost and by Tuesday the first arrests were being made. Information was gathered from various sources.

Many well known faces had been recognised over the course of the riots by a number of senior serving officers. Together with information from police informants a list of names began to emerge. A few of those involved could not help opening their mouths, usually under the influence of alcohol, in front of others who were prepared to give names to the police. Other witnesses picked out individuals at identity parades. A number of house searches were carried out, particularly in the New Town and High Town areas.

George Fowler was arrested and brought to Court from the Bute hospital. He was being treated for head injuries sustained, he claimed, after having been knocked down by the fire engine. It transpired that he was the only civilian treated at the hospital.

On the Wednesday the first cases were heard by Luton Magistrates but not before some embarrassment to the authorities. A minimum of two Magistrates were required for a hearing and only one had turned up. It then took almost as long to locate a second Magistrate as it did to dispose of the cases. When details of this became public it caused general amusement in the town for it had only been a few weeks previously that the entire bench had turned out to listen to details of an illegal betting case. There were also suggestions that Magistrates were in no great hurry to sign warrants. By the Saturday thirty cases had been heard. During the next week a further nine arrests were made, including George Heley, who was taken into custody at Chatham before being handed over to Luton police. He made his appearance in Court with a heavily bandaged head.

The Town Clerk had anticipated a lot more arrests but they never materialised. It seemed clear that many ordinary people who had been involved and had let events get the better of them, were lying low in the days following the riot and friends and work colleagues were not

Group photograph of representatives of Luton Borough Police Force and the six other Forces who were engaged in quelling the riots. In the centre of the front row is Chief Constable Griffin, next-but-one to his left Inspector Janes and next-but-one again Inspector Hunt. In civilian clothes on the right, with bandaged head is PC Sear and next to him, head also bandaged, PC Wood.

W. H. Cox/Source: T. Madigan

Where They Burnt The Town Hall Down

125

Luton Hoo Park, 27th July 1919. The Drumhead Memorial Serivce finally takes place with twenty thousand people in attendance. Lady Wernher can be seen with the walking stick. Source: Luton Museum Service

prepared to hand them over to the police.

A total of thirty-nine men and women were remanded in custody and sent to Bedford and Northampton prisons to await trial at Luton Borough Court. For the authorities it was a scant return from the hundreds of people who had been directly involved in the riots.

The trial of the accused men and women opened at Luton Borough Court on Wednesday 30th July 1919. Long before the proceedings began large crowds had gathered in Stuart Street, Dunstable Place and other streets en route from the railway station to witness the arrival of the defendants by train from Bedford. A large number of policemen were also on duty particularly at all the court entrances, at various points in the building and in the adjoining streets. A long queue had formed in the hope of gaining admittance to the proceedings but public seats were at a premium due to lack of space in the courtroom and only a handful gained entry.

For the trial the dock had been removed and the accused sat in four rows of seats across the court and behind their defending counsel. They were separated from the public by two rows of police officers. The rest of the seats were taken by witnesses and pressmen.

Conducting the case for the prosecution was the Town Clerk, William Smith, who 'presumed it was the wish of the Council to act on their behalf with all the force and power he might be able to exert'. The defence was conducted by Mr H. W. Lathom who represented twenty of the arraigned and Mr C. Barber who had been engaged by the DS&S to hold a watching brief for a further ten! Lathom was the leading advocate in the town and was the same gentleman who had precipitated the election riot of 1895 when he had swapped sides. Presiding over the bench was Mr R. S. Thompson the senior magistrate together with Messrs F. J. Brown, F. Beecroft, C. H. Osborne, G. Ordish, W. J. Mair and M. W. Janes.

The Town Clerk's opening statement lasted for almost an hour and summarised the events that had taken place on the peace day afternoon and night. In the course of his address Smith managed to lay blame for the trouble at the feet of Labour supporters, Bolsheviks and the press and contended that all of those who had taken part in the riot were drunk. In his summation he said 'It is the most lamentable event Luton has ever experienced and there was absolutely no good whatever for any such event at all. If these people had a legitimate grievance they are not entitled first of all to convert themselves into a riotous crowd, and finally to injure men who were endeavouring to perform their duty, especially firemen ... I am going to ask the Bench to send every man and woman for trial, and let them experience the weight of the law and learn for once in their lifetime that there is a superior power to a crowd which assembles in the street and loses its head and is animated throughout, not by local grievances, but by Bolshevism, anarchy and rebellion of the very worst type'.

Pointing out that the law regarded such conduct at night as being more serious than in the day he continued 'It may be of some satisfaction to the defendants to know that crime of this description merits and receives almost the most severe punishment the law inflicts with the exception of the death sentence. I mention that because I think it is my duty to let people know what the consequences will be if any repetition or attempt to repeat the operations of this particular night is made. For such actions as the demolition of buildings the extreme penalty is Penal Servitude For Life and that is a nice prospect for anybody to have in front of him'.

The Town Clerk went on to express his admiration of the bravery, personal courage, coolness and the intrepid manner in which Chief Constable Griffin dealt with the proceedings together with his men, the special constables and the fire brigade. He went on 'If there is any thought in the mind of any person that they intend to repeat

Luton Court House, Stuart Street.
(Source: Luton Central Library)

this operation there is a force of military immediately and instantly available, armed with the requisite ammunition, and on the next occasion we shall not have the slightest hesitation in applying that force, and the results so far as individuals are concerned will be much more serious than they were on the last occasion'.

Before resuming his seat Smith emphasised that none of his observations were intended in the slightest degree as any reflection on the discharged soldiers and sailors. He had the greatest admiration for every man who had served his country and did their duty, but that was not a reason why they should seek to govern on their return. They formed only a portion of the community and while their wishes and requirements should obviously receive consideration they alone could not decide what should be done.

The witnesses were then called to give their evidence. Frederick Rignall was first and before his testimony began a moment of light relief was brought in to the proceedings when Smith said,

'I may say, for the information of the Bench, that Rignall is only one of fifty-one witnesses who will be called.'

'Then we will not get done before lunch?' Lathom enquired causing laughter in the courtroom. The Town Clerk was unmoved and countered, 'We will not, nor by lunch time tomorrow.'

Chief Constable Griffin was next to give evidence and describing the events of the afternoon said,

'The crowd was horrible. It was a crowd of maniacs and the women were as violent as the men.'

Smith drew more laughter when he said,

'I shall have to change my opinion about women.'

Doctor Archibald gave his evidence followed by a number of police officers including Inspectors Hunt and Janes who gave more specific testimony against the individual defendants.

The proceedings were temporarily brought to a halt when Ephraim Gore leapt to his feet and looking wildly at the windows shouted,

'I can see them coming. Oh, yes here they come.'

He had to be held down before appearing to collapse and Inspector Janes carried him from the courtroom but both returned a short time later.

With the completion of the prosecution's evidence Smith suggested that the defendants' cases should be heard individually. Lathom having no objection to this rose to his feet to address the court.

'Everybody was impressed with the great sense of degradation which had fallen over the town,' he said, 'and the great sense of sorrow that to live in Luton should now be a byword in England simply because they did not know how to conduct themselves on a day when everybody should have acted with sobriety and quietness.'

Lathom, on behalf of himself and Mr Barber, joined with the Town Clerk in thanking the police in carrying out their duties in very difficult circumstances. He continued,

'The only sorrowful thing was that this did not apply to another public body in the three or four weeks before the trouble took place, when as everybody knew they were expecting trouble. The town was palpably seething with trouble and there was such as thing as preventing it by tact.'

The police had shown marvellous patience said Lathom, in the face of abuse and assault and if some had been shown by Luton Corporation there would need have been none of the trouble. They could keep the peace at Dunstable, where he lived, but not at Luton.

There was only time to deal with three of the accused before the court was adjourned at 8.00pm. There was an enormous crowd outside the courthouse who greeted the defendants with a huge cheer as they emerged before being driven away by bus to the railway station and returned to Bedford and Northampton jails.

The second day's proceedings began at 10.00am and lasted until 7.30pm. The court heard a graphic description of the riots given by Chief Officer Andrew. Several battered helmets were produced as evidence of the ferocity of the attacks on the firemen. The majority of the day was taken up with the cases of eleven more defendants.

Friday began with another lengthy statement from the Town Clerk. He had, he said, considered the cases of the women who had been charged with rioting and larceny. Recognising that they had suffered mental strain and stress while awaiting trial Smith said he was prepared to withdraw the charge of rioting from these cases and proceed with larceny only. However he made it clear his decision was not to be taken as any sign of weakness on his part.

Nineteen cases were heard including the cases of larceny and the court adjourned at 8.00pm. Saturday saw the five remaining cases completed by lunch time. The four days' proceedings had lasted just over twenty-seven hours.

Before the Court was closed on the Friday a presentation was made to Chief Constable Griffin by the Town Clerk. He was given a framed photograph and ebony walking stick on behalf of the police officers from the other forces whom he had commanded during the days after the riot.

Of the accused, twenty-eight were committed for trial at Bedford Assizes, of whom fifteen were granted bail. Ten were found guilty of larceny and one was discharged but ordered to be bound over for one year.

The party that Lady Wernher had offered to hold for the ex-servicemen duly went ahead on 16th August at Luton Hoo. A banner strung across the Park Street entrance emblazoned with the single word 'Welcome' greeted nearly six thousand men and their partners. They were treated to an afternoon of athletic events and a cricket match between the DS&S and Comrades versus Luton Hoo and unattached ex-servicemen! The Hoo team triumphed by forty-one runs to twenty-five. Four large marquees had been erected and food and drink were served throughout the afternoon.

One special event was greeted with great excitement when it was announced that some of the invited guests of Lady Wernher would take part in a special sack race. The event was won by Lord Louis Mountbatten.

Once again Lady Wernher was the champion of the ex-servicemen, so much so that on 24th September the DS&S invited her to run as a candidate for them at the forthcoming Municipal elections. There was even some speculation that she should be made Mayor. Lady Wernher politely declined the DS&S invitation and the following day married Lord Ludlow after the best kept society secret of the year

The Council held their usual meeting on 4th September and attending for the first time since riot week was Henry Impey. Addressing his colleagues, he told them that he had come to the meeting against medical orders as he was still suffering from poor health. Impey said that he proposed to hold the office of Mayor until his successor was elected in November and then he would resign from the Council. He went on to praise the Town Clerk and a number of the other Councillors for standing by him and talked about some of the meetings he had held prior to Peace Day. His statement meandered on for some time and was occasionally rather incoherent. Impey was obviously a very sick man. When he finally finished his address he was received in silence.

The only other item that came under discussion was a letter from the Labour Party calling for those responsible for the decision to refuse Wardown Park to resign. It produced some rather blunt and outspoken comments from those Councillors who wished to be exonerated from any blame but others felt they should all stand together even though it was clear misunderstandings and mistakes had been made. A resolution was passed to take no action on the letter.

The children of the town finally had their Peace Day festivities, over two days in September. Six thousand older children were entertained on Thursday, the 19th and three thousand younger children the following day. The Commemorative Medals had been presented by the wife of Councillor Staddon on a tour of the town schools earlier in the week. On a warm and sunny Thursday, the schoolchildren, marshalled by Chief Constable Griffin and a number of his officers, assembled in the town centre to march to Luton Hoo Park. Once again Lady Wernher had come to the rescue with her offer of use of the Park to cater for the large numbers. Her only disappointment was that she was unable to be present. Crowds lined the route as the children, wearing their medals, carrying flags and many dressed in costume, made their way to the Hoo led by the Red Cross Band. The procession, over a mile in length then proceeded into the Park where they were treated to food and drink at lunch time followed by inter-school sports in the afternoon. The children were then entertained to side-shows before they were given tea. At 7.00pm parents began to arrive and the crowd of around twenty-five thousand watched a fireworks display to round off the day.

On the Friday the younger children were presented with their medals before being entertained at the town's various cinemas. They were treated to food and drink and performances given by Punch and Judy shows and other entertainers. The children's two days of Peace celebrations were a huge success, albeit that they were two months late.

Bedford Assizes were opened at the Shire Hall on Thursday the 16th October 1919 but it was not until just after 4.00pm on the Friday afternoon that the trial of the rioters began.

Amazing scenes had been witnessed earlier in the morning at Luton Midland railway station as people thronged the platform awaiting the 9.02am train for Bedford. The railway authorities had provided a special carriage for the use of the police and prosecution witnesses which was standing in the sidings and was hitched up to the train as it pulled in from St. Pancras. A considerable number of friends of the prisoners were in the other carriages of the train as it made its way to Bedford station. The procession from the station made its way to the Shire Hall attracting huge interest from Bedfordians on the way.

The presiding judge, Sir Frederick Arthur Greer, was one of the newer High Court Judges and he was making his first round of circuit duties. Seven counsel were engaged on the cases. The prosecution was represented by Mr Hollis Walker KC assisted by Mr J. F. Eales KC who were briefed by Town Clerk, William Smith. Acting for the defence were Mr C. E. Dyer KC, Sir Ryland Adkins MP, Mr Bernard Campion, Mr H. B. Drysdale Woodcock and Mr J. P. Stimson who were instructed by Messes Lathom and Barber.

At 4.15pm the fifteen prisoners who had been given bail were called upon to surrender to the Court. The proceedings were immediately held up for almost thirty minutes when John Henry Good failed to answer the summons. It was known that Good had been in the building earlier but he could not be found. Eventually the Judge decided enough time had been wasted and ordered the trial to proceed without Good and that he would issue a warrant for his arrest.

The Jury had finally been sworn in after two men had been discharged, one who was in military uniform and a second who advised the Judge that he could not hear very well as he was rather deaf. The prisoners were then brought into Court. Those who had been brought from Bedford Prison were placed in the dock while the remainder stood in the balcony immediately behind with a police guard. The accused pleaded not guilty to all the counts in the indictment. It was 5.10pm before all the preliminaries were completed and Mr Hollis Walker stood to open the case for the prosecution.

Walker had hardly begun to speak before he was interrupted by Judge Greer. The judge said that in view of a late sitting the previous night he did not propose to go beyond 5.30pm and all the defendants would remain in custody during the course of the trial. This raised an objection from Mr Campion who said that a number of the accused should be let out on bail but he was overruled by the judge. Before the Court rose it was announced that Good had surrendered and Judge Greer agreed to let him be heard the following morning.

On the Saturday morning Good took the stand. A plea was made on his behalf that his absence had been a case of sheer stupidity. He had been in Court on the Friday morning but had been told, by someone who was not in authority, that there was no chance of his case being heard. He had then wandered off a short distance before being found. Judge Greer accepted the defence counsel plea but again proceedings were delayed to allow one of the Jury to be excused from duty as his

**Children's day of Peace celebrations 19th September 1919. Passing Why Axe Ye'
cottage in Park Street on their way to Luton Hoo Park.** Source: Luton Central Library

wife had died the previous night.

With the resumption Mr Hollis Walker presented the full story of the `outburst which took place at Luton and converted the celebration of peace into a time of outrage, fire and personal injury.

Frederick Rignall was the first witness and he was in the box for over an hour. He was cross-examined by Mr Drysdale Woodcock who concentrated on the seething discontent that had existed in the town due to the ex-servicemen's belief that they had been overlooked in the peace festivities. Woodcock questioned Rignall over the Mayor's banquet and the suggestion that discharged servicemen were 'invited to come on buying a fifteen shilling ticket for this banquet that was to celebrate their winning the war'. This drew an instant reaction from Hollis Walker.

`Don't talk such nonsense. There was no evidence that this banquet was to celebrate the winning of the war, and I protest against this.'

Judge Greer interjected with a question of his own,

`Surely nobody would suggest a Town Hall banquet at which some would be expected to pay?'

Amid considerable laughter Woodcock replied that this was the suggested case at Luton.

Further questioned Rignall said he did not know if tickets were offered to ex-servicemen to buy but agreed that the organisation of the banquet and the refusal of Wardown Park created a good deal of ill-feeling among the ex-servicemen.

Finally Woodcock asked Rignall to express his opinion as a resident of the town as to whether if the festivities, subsequently provided by Lady Ludlow for the ex-servicemen, had been organised by the Town Council 'we should have been here on this sad business'. Judge Greer wanted to know the purpose of this question. Woodcock said that he might suggest to the jury that if they felt bound to find the defendants guilty of riot they might also find that the conduct of the Mayor and Corporation was so provocative that the jury might be inclined to make a strong recommendation to the judge in dealing with the accused. Judge Greer replied that while he understood counsel's position he could not allow this line of cross-examination.

Chief Constable Griffin was in the witness box for just under an hour and was followed by Chief Officer Andrew and Dr Archibald.

The evidence for the prosecution concerning the charges against each of the accused began on the Saturday afternoon and with the majority of the defendants undergoing cross-examination it was Tuesday afternoon before all the evidence had been heard. Hollis Walker then asked to put William Smith into the witness box to give evidence relating to the Mayor's banquet and other matters raised in the earlier cross-examination of Rignall and Griffin. The judge however ruled that further testimony was irrelevant to the issue.

When the court rose on Tuesday evening the defence had only presented the evidence of six defendants and it was not until 1.00pm on Thursday that the case for the defence was completed. Considerable discussion between Judge and counsel then took place over what form the final summing up should take. After the luncheon adjournment Judge Greer announced that it would be the most expedient way to take each case individually.

The defence counsel asked the jury to consider that there was no evidence of a riot up to 4.00 o'clock in the afternoon. They said that one of the essentials of a 'modern' riot was the assembly of a number of individuals whose aim was the deliberate purpose of assisting one another in the production of turmoil and, argued counsel, there was no evidence that this was the case. Judge Greer asked if their submission was that no riot took place even though the Town Hall had been destroyed? Defence counsel's reply was that the events of the day could be divided into two parts and up to 4.00pm it was all innocent.

For the prosecution Mr Hollis Walker said to the jury that if it was not a riot when a crowd became angry and noisy, booed and yelled for the Mayor and Town Clerk, talked of rushing the Town Hall and then did, smashing everything they could lay their hands on inside, it was difficult to know what a riot was.

Judge Greer then began his summation. He had no doubt he said that July 19th was a date that was engraved on the memory of everybody who was in Luton on that day. No one, he believed, thought that there was a concerted conspiracy by the defendants or anybody to create trouble, destroy the Town Hall or physically harm the police or firemen. Unfortunately that was not enough to justify finding the prisoners not guilty of rioting. If having assembled together for a purpose that was in itself innocent, they started to become riotous and committed numerous breaches of the peace creating a sense of fear in reasonably-minded people, they were guilty of taking part in a riot.

No doubt said the Judge that by the time the end of the procession passed the Town Hall some of the rougher elements had got together and imagined they had grievances against the Mayor. 'We are not trying the Mayor of Luton here' he continued 'and we know nothing whatever of whether the grievance the people had was well or ill founded. It does not matter, because there are recognised peaceful methods by which people who have a grievance can make that grievance known. The fact you have a grievance, even if it is a good one, is no justification at all for riotous assembly and behaviour, and I think perhaps you will say the Mayor was wise and the officers who were looking after him were wise to see he went to some safe and secret place and remained there until the trouble was over. You have to consider the kind of language that was used. Is that the language of people who wanted him to make a speech or explanation and listen to him, or was it the language of people who were angry and just in the state of mind to commit a breach of the peace and create terror in the minds of other citizens?' The judge continued that riotous conduct was like a disease that passed from one to another very quickly through a crowd and once begun it was difficult to hold a crowd in control. There was no question that when the crowd rushed the Town Hall they had got beyond that control and it was his view that there was ample evidence on which it could be found that the riot in Luton began from the time the crowd started to call out in abusive language for the Mayor. He also said that he had very little doubt that the majority of the crowd who caused the damage in the evening were also present in the afternoon.

'The scenes that happened were an absolute disgrace to those who took part in them. People seemed to have gone mad and thought the best way in which they could show their criticism of the action of the authorities, including the Pension Ministry, with which Luton had nothing whatever to do, was to destroy the town's property and injure their own servants — the police and the firemen. The seriousness of it could not for one moment be disputed.'

The Judge then warned the jury to be prepared for a long day as he intended to sit late. Rapid progress was made in the afternoon in reaching verdicts but even though the court sat until 9.20pm nine cases remained to be dealt with the following day and the proceedings finally came to an end just before 4.00pm on the Friday.

Judge Greer closed the Assizes with these statements,

To Mr Charles Griffin, Chief Constable of the Borough of Luton: 'I desire to congratulate you as Chief Constable on the admirable way in which you tackled this extremely difficult problem, which so suddenly presented itself to you on July 19th. I wish you to tender to your Inspectors and all the members of your Force, which so admirably and courageously seconded your efforts, my sincere congratulations, not perhaps to them so much as to the town of Luton for having for the protection of the Ratepayers such admirable men in their service. I think they deserve the very best that can be said of them'.

(The Judge's words would be issued in the form of a Commendation Certificate to every officer who took part in the riots.)

To Mr Alexander Andrew, Chief Officer of the Luton Fire Brigade: 'I desire also to convey through Chief Officer Andrew my appreciation of the admirable and courageous service which he gave to the public on this occasion, and also to ask him to convey to his men my very deep sense of the admirable and courageous way in which they performed their duties in this terrible night in July'.

Jude Greer offered the Jury the thanks of Bedfordshire for their public service, rendered without reward, in coming to the verdicts of these difficult cases and he exempted them from further service for the next ten years.

Of the twenty-eight defendants tried, the Jury convicted nineteen who were sent to prison for varying terms except for two, who were bound over to keep the peace, while nine were acquitted.

Epilogue

The Town Hall ruins were demolished in August 1919 and a hoarding was put up around the perimeter of the site. Apart from official announcements no advertisements were allowed on the hoarding.

On 10th December 1922 the Town Council together with William Smith and Frederick Rignall and a vast crowd were present at the unveiling ceremony, performed by Lady Ludlow, of the War memorial commemorating Luton's dead in the Great War. It had been raised in George Street in front of the empty space left by the Town Hall ruin and on the spot where, a hundred years earlier, the large chestnut tree had stood in front of Cross Hill farm.

The Memorial, built of Portland stone, consisting of a plinth, body and podium was designed by Sir Reginald Blomfield RA, the podium surmounted by an eight foot tall bronze statue of 'Peace' sculpted by Sir Hamo Thorneycroft RA. One thousand two hundred and eighty-six names of the dead of First World War were inscribed on the four sides of the main body.

From 1919 the Council carried out the day-to-day running of Luton's affairs from temporary offices located in the Carnegie library and the Plait Halls but financial constraints postponed any plans for a new Town Hall.

In 1929 however they decided the time was right to consider having a new building. Visits were made to look at Municipal buildings in other towns but they had little success in making a decision on the style of building they required. What became apparent however was that other local authorities had run competitions to find a design and the Council decided to follow suit and appointed Sir A. Brumwell Thomas FRIBA to act as their assessor.

Thomas considered the site of the old Town Hall was unsuitable due to its great variation in levels, limitation of area and proximity to commercial buildings. A number of other sites were suggested including the Moor. After viewing them all Thomas decided that despite its limitations the original site was after all the best available. After ascertaining the requirements of its various departments the Council set a spending limit of £200,000 for the building. One feature to be incorporated into tie design was accommodation for a clock for which £1,250 had been left .7o the Council in the will of the late Alderman Albert Wilkinson.

By February 1930 the competition was ready and in March announcements were inserted in a number of building journal=. The closing date for the competition was set for 31st July with a £500 first prize to be awarded for the best design and other cash award; for Three runners up. A total of eighty-six entries were submitted and the winning architects were Messrs. Bradshaw Gass & Hope FFRIBA of Bohm.

In 1931 before the project had even got under way financial problems were encountered. The Ministry of Health who were providing a _Dan to the Council considered the design to be too generous for them and were only prepared to sanction the loan if the plans were modified aria the cost reduced. The problem was solved by removing the large public assembly hall from the proposed design as it already included a smaller hail. National financial restraints further delayed the project and finally in May 1934 the plans were submitted to the Royal Fine Arts Commission a for their approval.

The Commission did not like the design and in particular the clock tower which was set back from the front of the building. The Commission wanted the tower brought forward to a central position on the main frontage. The architects were unhappy pointing out that their design had been chosen in open competition by the Council. As a result a sub-committee of the two parties was formed and they agreed on the modifications required.

The Town Council finally approved the new design in June 1934. The building was then put out to contract and the tender of £107,640.12s.4d from Messrs. E. D. Winn & Co. Ltd was accepted. On the 30th May 1935 the Foundation Stone was laid by Mayor John Harrison and Alderman G. Wistow Walker, Chairman of the Municipal Building Committee.

The building, faced in Portland Stone was completed in 1936. It was

George Street from the Town Hall site at the beginning of construction of th6 new Town Hall. Source: Luton Centra. Liurary

The Duke of Kent officially opens the New Town Hall on 28th October 1936.

Luton News/Source: Luton Central Library

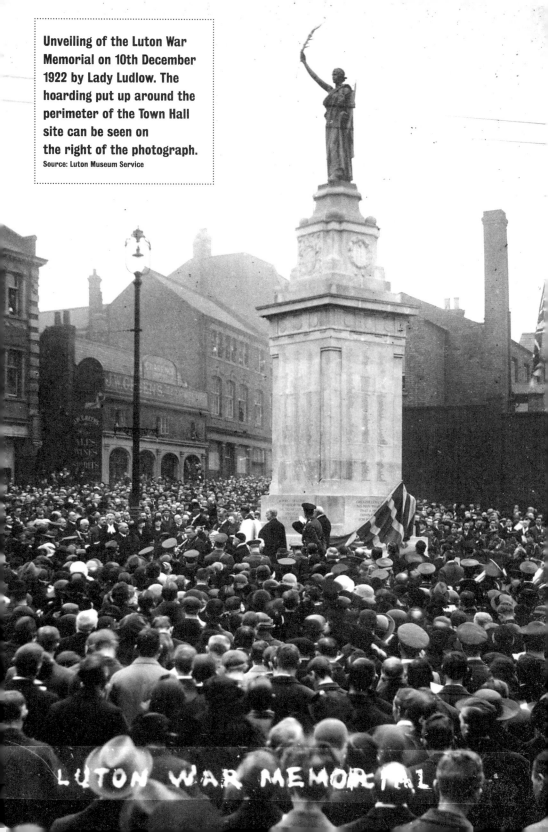

Unveiling of the Luton War Memorial on 10th December 1922 by Lady Ludlow. The hoarding put up around the perimeter of the Town Hall site can be seen on the right of the photograph.
Source: Luton Museum Service

LUTON WAR MEMORIAL

no great surprise to Lutonians to learn that fireproof materials were used in its internal construction.

On Wednesday 28th October 1936 the official opening of the new Town Hall was performed by His Royal Highness, The Duke of Kent.

The New Town Hall.
Source: Luton Museum Service

TOWN HALL, LUTON.   G.5871

Conclusions

The First World War brought about a permanent change to the industry infrastructure in Luton. Hat manufacture continued but loss of its export trade dealt a large blow and it would never regain its former prominence. In contrast, the engineering firms, enticed to the town by the pre-war New Industries Committee, grew rapidly as they expanded and adapted to meet munitions and other war contracts. This expansion generated an influx of workers into the town and with it came a large rise in membership of Trade Unions. Luton reflected the national trend which had seen the total membership reach nearly eight million by 1919, almost double what it had been at the outbreak of war. Government recognition of the Labour Party and Trade Union movement as partners in the war economy had given them a position of some strength. When they felt there was injustice workers, led by their shop stewards, were not slow in taking action. The `Munitions Strike' of May 1917 was a typical example and Luton was affected by a national labour dispute for the first time. Although this strike lasted ten days it was the local mass walkout over food distribution in 1918 that had the greater repercussions in the town.

The food problems had produced genuine feelings of inequality and injustice among the working class in Luton at a time when sacrifices were required from everyone. This together with claims of profiteering and the inadequacies levelled at the Food Control Committee presented the Town Council with the biggest challenge to its authority it had ever had to endure. Faced with a prolonged strike led by the Luton Trades and Labour Council, the local authority was pressured not only into acceding to their demands but were forced into the ignominy of seeing one of their colleagues resign from a Committee.

There was never any proof that Alderman Edwin Oakley was ever guilty of self interest while a member of the Food Committee but the rumours were enough and he took the only decision possible. It was one that would have been unheard of before the war. His resignation only engendered a perception in the town that some Councillors were lining their pockets while men on the front lines were dying or suffering privation in the trenches.

The end result was a huge gulf that developed between the Town Council, seemingly living in the past and seeped in its middle class Liberalism and a working class population for the first time beginning to be aware of pride in their own social class.

Not all members of the Corporation were seen in a bad light. Foremost among them was Alderman John Staddon. The only

Edwin Oakley photographed in the Mayor's Parlour of the Town Hall during his third and last term in 1907. Behind him hang a number of framed documents among which was a Papal Bull, a letter, written from Pope Adrian 4th to the Vicar of Shefford in the 12th Century. All were destroyed in the Town Hall fire.

T. G. Hobbs/Source: Luton Museum Serivce

Conservative on the Council, he never let politics get in the way of common sense as he demonstrated as chairman of the Food Control Committee. His strength of character had been evident in the Munitions Strike during his term as Mayor, when he refused to let the Military intervene in the dispute locally and kept control within the hands of the Council. Of all the members of the Corporation he was the one who was able to empathise most with the working class in the town. Events may well have turned out differently if Staddon had been Mayor!

The early months of 1919 saw the Council taking decisions in their meetings that in hindsight seem perplexing and only exacerbated the anger and frustration many Lutonians had in their Corporation.

Wardown House and Park was put forward as the ideal site for the proposed maternity hospital. It had been Edwin Oakley of course who had helped to secure the estate for the town. The debate about its future lasted until May when it was finally announced that the idea had been dropped. Pressure from both the public and local press had secured its survival as the town's premier leisure facility. The other issue that was discussed at Council meetings along with the use for Wardown were the proposals for the Peace Celebrations.

The formation of a Peace Committee, first suggested by the Town Clerk, was flawed in one significant respect, there was no representation from the various organisations within the town. It was comprised of Council members only. No move was made to unite the various bodies even though opportunities presented themselves and no lessons appear to have been learned from the problems faced by the Food Committee a year earlier. If anything the gulf between the Council and the townspeople was driven even wider. Yet surprisingly no objection seems to have been made over the constitution of the Peace Committee.

From the outset the Council made it clear that the level of celebrations would be limited by the funds available. The raising of a halfpenny rate to pay for the programme caused disagreement among Councillors some of whom felt they money should come from private sources. It did not help either that rumours were bandied about suggesting misappropriation of money from dormant war funds. There can be no doubt however that a Peace Committee consisting of representatives from the Corporation, the ex-servicemen and the Trades and Labour Council would have brought about a sense of unity and with it quite possibly substantial funds from the private sector for the programme of celebrations. It is a matter of conjecture as to whether or not some of the decisions that the Council took were born out a sense of pique, a result of the demands made of them in the final year of the war.

Reaction to the Mayor's Banquet only increased the tension that was developing even further. Not only did it offend the women in the town, due to it being a men only occasion, but also the ex-servicemen, who took great exception to the fact that guests invited by the Mayor could go free while everyone else had to pay fifteen shillings. Tickets were made available to the ex-servicemen's organisations but few men could contemplate paying so much for admission. With the small number of ex-servicemen who were being asked to take part in the procession it is no surprise that their overriding feeling was one of feeling snubbed having fought to bring about the peace. The fact that only a small number of the free tickets were ever taken up and the venue was changed from the Plait Halls to the smaller Town Hall assembly room was surely proof that the arrangements for the banquet totally missed their mark. At Bedford Assizes, Frederick Rignall stated that as far as he was aware the banquet was cancelled at the last minute although no other evidence appears to corroborate his. The arrangements in Luton can be compared to other towns such as Cambridge where three thousand three hundred and fifty ex-servicemen attended a dinner on Peace Day and at Oxford where nearly four thousand men marched through the town before dining in the Municipal buildings and college halls.

Anger at the proposals for Peace celebrations were compounded even further when it became apparent that nobody had considered the children. It was not until this was highlighted in the local press that the Council acted by arranging for medals to be presented, and festivities arranged. Once again though money was a problem and it was only through John Staddon, in his position as a director of Vyse and Co who offered to pay, that the medals got the go ahead. By the time the Council acted, though, time was short and it was no surprise that the manufacturers could not deliver the medals for Peace Day. In the Council's defence they were not to know that the date would be brought forward by two weeks. The Council also argued that many children would not be present during the summer holidays and that a day in term time should be made available for a party which was what subsequently happened. Again though it is interesting to compare what happened in Luton with other towns.

In Aldershot, five thousand children were entertained on Peace

Day, in Cambridge eight thousand attended a party on the Sunday and in Bradford children were given commemorative medals and entertained on the Friday and Saturday.

The DS&S request to use Wardown Park for the Drumhead Memorial Service was submitted on 7th July. The application was placed before the Tolls and Municipal Buildings Committee of whom six members constituted the majority of the Parks Committee, who administered Wardown. The Watch Committee ratified the decision to reject the request later the same evening. In doing so thirteen members of the Council became involved in the decision. With regard to bye-laws that existed the decision to reject the request has to be considered

The Peace Day Medal presented to all the Luton school children in late September when their celebrations were finally held.

Source: Luton Museum Service

correct based on the premise that the DS&S represented only some of the ex-servicemen. The question that has to be asked though is why was the request not put before the full Council.

Town Clerk William Smith suggested that the DS&S required an answer as quickly as possible and the next Council meeting was not scheduled until after Peace Day. However it took three days to call an extraordinary meeting. What does seem surprising is that a meeting was not called when considering that correspondence between Smith and Henry Cooper of the DS&S went back and forth over a period of five days until the 9th July before the DS&S finally accepted the refusal of Wardown. The full Council could have met on the 8th July to discuss the request; conceivably the outcome nay have been different. John Staddon made it clear shortly afterwards that he for one was disappointed with the decision. (A few years earlier, Staddon, as chairman of the Parks Committee, had been responsible for securing Sunday band concerts in Wardown Park, in the face of strong opposition.)

The Town Clerk, William Smith, was the most influential member of the Corporation. A man skilled at his job and someone who played everything by the rule book, he had become by the summer of 1919 extremely unpopular in the eyes of many Lutonians. His defence of the self employed during the war tribunals did nothing to endear him to

John Henry Staddon photographed in 1915 during his first term as Mayor. On the left of the group is William Smith, the Town Clerk, and standing in the centre of the doorway is Frederick Rignall, the Mayor's Sergeant at Arms and Macebearer.

F. Thurston|Source: Luton Museum Service

the general public. Once again they perceived protection of the middle class to the detriment of the working class. He earned the nickname 'Bully Smith' the origin of which probably came about with his cross-examination of men applying for exemption at the tribunal. Smith was always to be seen at the side of the incumbent Mayor. Tall in his wig and gown he was the personification of authority, so much so that many people were under the belief that it was Smith who ran the affairs of the town and made all the decisions. His role was only to offer advice but such was his ability and knowledge that some members of the Council were quite happy to let Smith have some influence in making their decisions. It is probable that one of them was Henry Impey.

It was Henry Impey's misfortune to be chosen as Mayor in one of the most traumatic years in the town's history. He was one of the least assertive members of the Council and lacked the character to impose his views on his colleagues. Hard working, he was not from the same mould as many of his colleagues but served the town well as a Councillor for a solid but undistinguished seventeen years. Essentially his only fault was to try and appease all parties in the build-up to Peace Day but one of the saddest aspects of the affair was the way he was subsequently treated. Lutonians and the local press wanted to lay the blame for the riot at someone's feet. In Impey's absence in the days that followed, his colleagues on the Council were quite happy to offer him up as the scapegoat. It did not matter that he was being advised to keep out of the town by the Town Clerk and the Chief Constable. His absence was seen as an admission of guilt. After all he was the head of the Borough and Chairman of the Peace Committee.

Henry Impey ultimately paid a price out of all proportion to anything he said or did. The riot shattered his health and he was virtually ostracised from Luton, the town where he was born and which he loved. His was the biggest human tragedy of the riots.

From their inception the DS&S set out with the intention of becoming the leading organisation for ex-servicemen both nationally and locally. In Luton they were much better organised than the Comrades due primarily to the efforts put in by their secretary Henry Charles Cooper. Their hatred of the Comrades and the need to be number one became an obsession. Even in October 1919 in the run up to the Municipal elections with candidates standing for both organisations the editorial of their DS&S Journal stated *'this Association which represents two thousand two hundred and fifty ex-servicemen of Luton, and therefore, by virtue of seniority and membership, is the representative body of ex-servicemen'*.

When it came to the Drumhead Memorial Service the DS&S were not prepared to organise one jointly with the Comrades, but were only prepared to send them an invitation. When they first made the decision to hold a service in May they chose Luton Hoo Park as the proposed venue. Why they changed their minds and requested Wardown Park two months later is unclear, although it has to be seen as the better venue. What is clear is that the DS&S assumed that the Council would give them permission and their request was only a formality, for they had their invitations printed and dated for July 3rd, two days before they applied for the use of Wardown. The DS&S were so entrenched in their feud with the Comrades, that even after the Council had explained why Wardown had been rejected, they were still not prepared to involve their fellow organisation in a joint request. There is little doubt that the Council would have given permission for such a request. By presenting the correspondence relating to Wardown to the press they further fostered the perception of a heartless, uncaring Council and brought the issue out into the open. The perception also grew over the years that the DS&S withdrew from the procession in protest over the Council's stand over Wardown. It was conveniently forgotten that the decision to withdraw was made by the parent Federation on a national basis and that the DS&S informed the Town Council on the same day they applied for the use of Wardown Park.

The Comrades had hardly any voice in any of the Peace programme disputes even though they were kept equally informed of the progress and decisions of the Council by Town Clerk William Smith. The one decision they did take, entering their contingent of ex-servicemen in the procession at the last minute left the DS&S seething with anger. Having initially withdrawn in support over Wardown, it was the Comrades who were cheered by the crowds as they led the Peace procession. It was an about turn that the DS&S found impossible to forget and it has to be considered that it was planned by the Comrades. The notice in The Saturday Telegraph, published on the Friday, was clear enough that Charles Strapps was preparing to enter the Jack Cornwell tableau even though at that stage no change of mind had been made. Strapps was a well known member of the Comrades and would have been aware of any decision that was going to be made. When the Municipal elections took place in November, Strapps was one of two candidates for the Comrades. The DS&S entered one candidate and in the editorial of their October 28th edition of their Journal they savaged their fellow organisation. *'It is fairly evident that we are up against some opposition, and rather unscrupulous at that, from our friends the Comrades ... But the Comrades, after all their protestations against the action of the Council, took part in the peace procession! ... What a farce to talk of co-operation when their every action is one of hostility and opposition!'* The eventual part that the Comrades took in the peace procession was a bitter pill for the DS&S to swallow.

How many of those eventually arrested were members of either of the ex-servicemen organisation? Unfortunately a definitive answer cannot be given but by looking at the representation of the accused, at both Luton Borough Court and Bedford Assizes some facts do emerge.

The DS&S claimed from the outset that none of those arrested were their members. At Luton Borough Court however they employed Mr C. Barber to hold a watching brief on their behalf for ten of the defendants. At the Assizes Barber instructed counsel who acted for nine of the accused, eight of whom were found guilty. This is no proof of course, but by implication just under half of those eventually found guilty were probably members of the DS&S. One ironic twist does emerge. George Heley, who took part in the procession as a member of the Comrades' Jack Cornwell Tableau, was represented at both trials by

Barber! The Comrades made no representation at either court sitting.

Luton saw the most serious of several riots that were clustered around the Peace Day celebrations. On the Saturday disturbances broke out at Coventry, Epsom, Salisbury and Bilston near Wolverhampton and shortly after at Swindon. There was looting and confrontation with the police and in Coventry, Swindon and Bilston the trouble continued until the Tuesday. They all involved ex-servicemen disillusioned with their treatment after being demobbed.

Neither was it a situation unique in Britain. On 21st July members of the Returned Soldiers League invaded the State Offices in Melbourne and demanded from the Australian Premier, Mr Lawson, the release of Returned Soldiers arrested after a confrontation on the Sunday night. Windows were broken, other damage caused and the Premier was assaulted.

Tension heightened in Luton as rumours began to circulate of impending trouble. At the annual general meeting of the DS&S on 20th January 1920 Henry Charles Cooper in his progress review for the year of 1919 spoke of the riot when he reported *'In the meantime the Committee had heard very disquieting rumours and every conceivable means of appealing to our own members to withhold from any severe action was taken advantage of'*. One of the ways they made their appeal was to place the two notices in the press on behalf of the DS&S and the Chief Constable. It is interesting that no notices were placed by the Comrades.

The events that took place on Peace Day evolved as much from misfortune, or good fortune depending on how you saw it, rather than through anything that had been pre-planned.

The speeches that were made in front of the Town Hall in the afternoon, aired grievances about pensions and other national issues. Nobody was heard to mention the issue of Wardown. It is therefore somewhat strange that there were calls for Impey and Smith to come out and address the crowd as they obviously had no influence on national issues.

The original objective of trying to find Impey when the Town Hall was rushed was quickly forgotten by the rioters when they entered the assembly room. There is no doubt that the vandalism that occurred here was based on the belief that the Mayor's banquet was going to be held in the room. Damage was caused in other parts of the Town Hall but not to the same extent.

It is doubtful that the appearance of Messrs. Clay and Mair to address the crowd around 6.30pm had much effect. Their appeals were being heard by crowds of bystanders; the troublemakers were by this time drinking in the pubs. However the story that grew that the 'Riot Act' had been read may well have been as a result of their appeal from the steps of the Town Hall, especially as they could not have been heard by many in the crowd.

In his account John Dony suggests that the police could have secured the town centre during the early evening as the crowd had dispersed. All the evidence however indicates that there was a crowd of around fifteen hundred people who remained in George Street all through this time. There was no way with his limited resources that Chief Constable Griffin could clear the street and in any case there was no trouble occurring at this time. There can be no doubt though that the crowd remained with the expectation that further trouble would break out. The hard-core of troublemakers who made their way into the crowds were able to find missiles easy to come by. Road repairs to one of the side streets had left a pile of rubble close to the town centre. Drink also played a large part in the evening. Many of those returning to George Street had spent the last four hours in public houses, although the main influx of people came from the fireworks display.

The start of the missile throwing does seem to have been planned to coincide with the lighting of the flares. This was purely vandalism and an expression of anger towards the Council. To damage the Town Hall was to damage them. The first real problem occurred when it was realised that entry could be gained through the smashed windows of the Food Office. Here the first fire was started. Ration books and coupons were used to fuel it and the crowd was also showered with coupons in what was a clear expression of the anger that the food distribution problems of the previous year had created in the town.

Second Officer Plummer and his firemen, though working under a hail of missiles, apparently had the fire under control. The failure of the assembly room internal hydrant was probably the most unfortunate event of the whole evening. The firemen lost their supply of water, and were forced to return to the station. In the time that passed before Chief Officer Andrew arrived with the engine the blaze had become re-established and a second fire had been started.

Andrew stated in evidence that the fire was easily containable but the appearance of the fire engine without police protection was an easy target for the excited crowd and it was at this stage that they let events take control of their actions. As Judge Greer said at Bedford Assizes rioting is infectious and it only required a few troublemakers to incite many in the crowd to involve themselves in the assault on the firemen without thinking of the consequences of their actions. With the fire brigade driven off there was nothing to stop fires taking hold in the wooden interior of the building. Other individuals who were clearly out to cause trouble saw there was nothing to stop them from throwing petrol and other flammable material on the blaze.

The police were never in a position to prevent serious trouble. The number of men under Chief Constable Griffin was never going to be sufficient to stop the rioting in the evening once it had started. It is clear that a few men took advantage during the riot to assault some of the policemen as a means of getting their own back on certain officers. The police made brave but futile charges to disperse the crowd which resulted in the majority of his men being injured and this was possibly Griffin's biggest mistake. If he had kept to a defensive plan and organised all his officers in and around the Town Hall it is conceivable that they would have prevented a lot of the intruders getting in and starting fires. They could also have offered protection to Chief Officer Andrew when he arrived with the fire engine at 11.00pm. Ultimately their action was confined to protection of the firemen later in the evening when they tried to prevent the fire from spreading.

Considering the ferocity of the baton charges and the violence that was used by both sides it seems incredible that there were no fatalities on the night.

Judge Greer throughout the trial at Bedford Assizes took the position that many of the issues were of the Town Council's own making. This was emphasised when he ruled that he would not allow the prosecution to call William Smith to elaborate further on the issues of the Mayor's banquet and Wardown. He considered enough had been heard already. He gave a fair and generally sympathetic hearing to the accused while paying attention to previous convictions. In the main the sentences he passed were relatively light. They certainly do not reflect the seriousness of the riot but then those found guilty were only charged with riot and/or assault. Nobody was charged with demolition of the Town Hall, no evidence was presented to support the charge. It was a far cry from the Luton Borough Court when Town Clerk William Smith demanded Penal Servitude for Life for those convicted of demolition.

Of the twenty-eight defendants at Bedford Assizes nine men were found not guilty and eighteen men and one woman found guilty. Their average age was thirty-six years old. All eighteen had served their country for varying periods during the war and ten of them had been wounded, some more than once. A few were suffering from 'shell shock', what would now be called post-traumatic stress disorder, and at times during the riot the excitement made them mentally unbalanced. Eight of them had previous criminal convictions, mostly petty, and were out looking for trouble. Well known to the longer serving police officers, their faces were easily recognisable on the night. Others just let the frenzy of the evening get the better of them.

When the Town Hall had been built the poorest parts of Luton could be found in New Town, Park Town and High Town. In 1919 this was still the case. Seventeen of the defendants came from these areas. Adelaide Terrace, off George Street, and Langley Place contained the worst slum property in the town. Four defendants lived in these two streets. The majority of those arrested were working class poor, a number of them petty criminals but many others could feel thankful that they were never brought to trial, encouraged by hundreds of law abiding citizens who were quite happy to stand by, cheer, laugh and dance as the Town Hall burnt down. As the years passed it is no wonder that the people of Luton wanted to forget the episode.

The Town Council must shoulder the larger share of the blame for the trouble that broke out on Peace Day. They had opportunities to heal the rifts that had developed with the general public during the war, but they never took them. Instead the bad feeling was allowed to fester. Their penny-pinching attitude toward the Peace Day celebrations was an anathema to people who had suffered five years of war, were still under the control of food rationing and were looking to a new beginning. The Council then aggravated the situation by snubbing the very men who had fought to bring about peace. However the ex-servicemen's organisations and in particular the DS&S could in no way claim that they were innocent of helping to create the seething tension that existed within the town in the days leading up to the celebrations.

That there had been talk of disrupting the Mayor's banquet was common knowledge in the town prior to Peace Day. There is no doubt that some form of disturbance, centred on the Town Hall, was talked of in the preceding days. Maybe just acts of vandalism. Possibly there was talk of setting fire to the old building, brave words spoken in the pubs or ex-servicemen's clubs, after a few drinks.

Judge Greer in his summing up at Bedford Assizes did not believe that the crowd had set out with the intention of burning down the Town Hall. In this assessment he was probably correct. But on the night of 19th July a combination of unfortunate circumstances contrived to allow small fires and an excited crowd to get totally out of control.

The Luton Peace Day Riots produced no winners. Social and economic unrest continued for a number of years resulting in the General Strike of 1926. The Town Council were left without Municipal buildings and had to operate from temporary offices for the next seventeen years. The DS&S were tarred with the accusation that it was their members who had started all the trouble of Peace Day. For this reason alone they could definitely claim they were the town's premier ex-servicemen's organisation.

Afterword

HENRY IMPEY

Returned to Luton twice during September to attend Council meetings. After the municipal elections in November 1919 he resigned from the Town Council. He and his wife left Harringay and moved to Milton and then Northampton before finally going to live at Sutton on Sea in Lincolnshire. Here he became an active member of the local Methodist church, a Justice of the Peace and a member of the Mabelthorpe and Sutton Urban District Council. While chairman of the Council he was taken seriously ill and died on 17th April 1930 aged 65. His body was conveyed to Luton for the last time and after a funeral service at Mount Tabor Church he was interred at the General Cemetery.

WILLIAM SMITH

Was still Town Clerk of Luton when he died on 7th January 1932. He had been suffering from a heart condition for two years. At the time of his death he was overseeing the plans for the building of the new Town Hall. The town was brought to a standstill on the day of his funeral when the funeral entourage made its way from the Carnegie Library (still being used as temporary home to the Council) to King Street Congregational Church. The Mayor and Town Councillors followed Frederick Rignall, still Sergeant at Arms, who carried the town mace draped in black. Smith was interred at the General Cemetery. (The position of Town Clerk was abolished in 1974.)

CHARLES GRIFFIN

Left Luton on 31st May 1920 after being appointed Chief Constable of Brighton and took up his new post on 5th June in charge of a force of two hundred men. On 11th May 1926, during the General Strike, there was a confrontation in Brighton between strikers and the police. Three hundred officers and special constables were pelted with bricks and stones. After calling for the strikers to disperse to no avail, Chief Constable Griffin led his men in a wedge formation and scattered them. Seventeen people were arrested and several police officers injured. He remained at Brighton until his retirement at the end of 1933. He died in Lincolnshire in 1960.

ALEXANDER ANDREW

As Chief Officer of Luton Fire Brigade he introduced new

fire fighting techniques and equipment. In 1924 a street fire alarm system was installed. (The last of these 'break the glass' alarms was removed in 1955.) In 1929 he introduced a new motor pump based on an American design which attracted considerable interest and was sometimes referred to as the `Andrew of Luton machine'. Andrew resigned on health grounds during 1941. In the same year the National Fire Service was formed.

HENRY CHARLES COOPER

Due to continuing ill health and on the advice of his doctor Cooper resigned from the DS&S on 12th April 1920. In the previous two years he had dealt with some six hundred pension cases of ex-servicemen and their dependants. He died in 1974.

The DS&S and the COMRADES

With changes to the DS&S membership rules and the government making revisions to the pensions system, much of the tension and aggression between them was reduced and the ex-servicemen's organisations began to show some unity from late 1919. They were helped by the involvement of Sir Douglas Haig in efforts to unify them. On 15th May 1921 in pouring rain, four men representing the Federation, the Comrades, the Association and the Officers Association (formed in 1920) each placed a laurel wreath at the base of the Cenotaph. Big Ben struck 9.00am and four buglers from the Foot Guards played the Last Post. The British Legion was born. On the Cenotaph lay another wreath containing the four badges of the old organisations.

ALBERT JOSEPH SEAR

Was promoted to the rank of Inspector of Luton Borough police force. During the Second World War he was awarded the George Medal when a parachute mine was dropped on Luton airport and landed in the roof of Percival Aircraft Ltd. Sear took charge as acting ARP incident officer and assisted, along with others, a naval Lieutenant in moving the mine to enable a second fuse to be removed. In the process the mine slipped and fell nine feet onto the factory floor. It failed to explode and the fuse was removed. Sear was later promoted Deputy Chief Constable and with amalgamation of the Luton force, retired as Superintendent of Beds. County Police.

FREDERICK JANES

Retired on 4th June 1937 from Luton Borough Police force with the rank of Chief Inspector. He had behind him forty-four years service.

HERBERT HUNT

Retired in January 1931 from Luton Borough Police force with the rank of Inspector. On 26th of the same month he was found dead, having committed suicide.

JOHN STADDON

Retired from the Town Council in 1923 after twenty-eight years' service but continued to serve on the Bedfordshire County Council. He remained on the Luton Magistrates Bench where he became affectionately known as 'Judge Staddon'. On 28th April 1938 he was presented with the Freedom of the Borough of Luton. Died 2nd June 1944 at the age of eighty-four, arguably the most influential and popular Councillor of his time.

EDWIN OAKLEY

Retired from the Town Council in 1920 having served continuously for thirty-seven years. Presented with the freedom of the Borough of Luton on April 5th 1921. Was still a Magistrate at the time of his death on 20th February 1930.

The Wernhers and Luton Hoo

In 1871, Julius Wernher, a twenty-one year old German engineer, arrived in South Africa. Over the next thirty years, the age of Victorian Imperialism on the African continent, Wernher became one of the most powerful and wealthiest of the 'Randlords', amassing his fortune from the diamond fields of Kimberley. On the way he became a close associate of Cecil Rhodes and Alfred Beit. It was with the latter that he founded `Wernher, Beit' in 1890, a mining and financial company that would be known world-wide. He was also made a Life Governor of De Beers. Wernher had come to England in 1884 and shortly after he met and in 1888 married Alice Sedgewick Manciewicz. Twelve years his junior of English and Polish decent, Alice was and would always be known as `Birdie'. The couple had three sons, Derrick born 7th June 1889, Harold born 16th January 1893 and Alexander born 18th January 1897.

In 1899 Wernher took out a lease on the vacant mansion and estate of Luton Hoo, just to the south of Luton, before purchasing the property for nearly £250,000 in 1903.

A house had been in existence from at least the thirteenth century and in 1762, John Crichton Stuart, the third Earl of Bute bought the estate and with it the Lordship of the Manor of Luton. Stuart decided to demolish the house and have a new one built. He engaged the foremost architect of the period, Robert Adam, to design it and at the same time Capability Brown carried out landscaping and enlargement of the estate.

The second Marquis of Bute, Stuart's grandson, succeeded to the title in 1814 and extensive alterations were carried out at the house. In 1843 disaster struck when fire ravaged the building,

destroying almost everything. The Marquis lost interest and decided to sell.

It was purchased by a wealthy Liverpool solicitor, John Shaw Leigh in 1848 and he immediately set about having the house restored and extended. On his death in 1871 the estate passed to his son J. Gerald Leigh and on his death four years later, to his wife. She subsequently married the Danish Ambassador to England, Christian de Falbe. With the death of Madame de Falbe in 1899 Luton Hoo remained unoccupied for a time until it was leased to Julius Wernher.

In 1905 he became Sir Julius and it was at this time that the interior of the house was being extensively redesigned, the work being completed in 1906 at a cost of £150,000.

The Wernhers were popular with Lutonians and they in turn took a great interest in the town's affairs. Whenever they drove through the town the three boys were always to be seen wearing straw boaters. Sir Julius, as Lord of the Manor, was happy to relinquish some of his medieval rights and as part of the 'Luton Corporation Act' in 1911 sold the freehold of the Corn Exchange to the Council.

On 21st May 1912 at the age of sixty-two Sir Julius Wernher died and was buried at the village of East Hyde near Luton Hoo. His funeral was a simple affair but even so five thousand townspeople lined the route. Lady Wernher was too upset to attend. Birdie was now Lady of the Manor. Always a strong character in her own right, the coming of the First

World War now gave her an outlet to display both this facet and her generosity. She contributed large sums to local charities and war funds. In 1914 Someries Chapel in the Luton Parish Church of St. Marys was restored at a cost of £6,000 in memory of Julius. In 1920 she presented eleven acres of the Hoo estate to the town, which became Luton Memorial Park, in memory of her son Alex.

On 25th September 1919 Birdie became Lady Ludlow when she married lawyer Henry Ludlow. He was however a totally different character to Julius and the marriage was not a happy one.

While riding in Luton Hoo park, Lord Ludlow was thrown from his horse and suffered concussion. Pneumonia set in and on 8th November 1922 he died. Even so through the twenties and thirties Birdie became one of society's leading hostesses, noted for her jewels and furs.

In early 1941 Birdie left Luton Hoo; it was taken on by her son Harold and she moved to Godalming. On 30th November 1945 at the age of eighty-three and after a long illness, Alice 'Birdie' Wernher died in a London nursing home.

Wardown House and Park

In July 1868, Frank Chapman Scargill, Luton solicitor and future chairman of the Board of Health, purchased from Robert How a farmhouse and land on the edge of Luton called Bramingham Shott. The farmhouse was demolished and Scargill proceeded to have a mansion built. Constructed in two stages it was completed in 1877. Adjoining land was purchased from John Crawley and incorporated into the estate and the original name was retained. Scargill left Luton in 1894 and he let the estate to B. J. H. Forder owner of a brick-making firm which had recently started work in Bedfordshire. Forder changed the name of the estate to Wardown, the name of a previous house he had lived at in Hampshire and in 1900 the estate was let to one of his partners, Halley Stewart. Stewart was the father of Sir Malcolm Stewart who founded the Stewartby Brick Company.

In 1902 Scargill sold Wardown House and the whole of the estate to three Luton businessmen for £15,500. Almost immediately they put the property back on the market at an asking price of £17,000. Offers were received from a religious order, recently banished from France, and the Town Council. The Council reached their purchase limit of £16,000 and just when it seemed the offer from the religious order would be accepted, Mayor Asher Hucklesby and Councillor Edwin Oakley, acting as private purchasers, stepped in and negotiated a price of £16,250. The sale was completed on 29th September 1903.

The two men then gave the Town Council the opportunity to purchase the estate from them for the same price. To the Council's credit they took up the offer and on 7th June 1904 became the new owners of Wardown House and Grounds. On July 8th 1905, Wardown Park was officially opened to the public and proved to be a tremendous success. The park was laid out with bowling greens, tennis courts and a cricket pitch and the lake was extended to facilitate rowing boats. Fetes and band concerts were held regularly in the summer and to 'go to Wardown' soon became the popular pastime.

The house was used as a restaurant, a hospital during the First World War and rented to Council employees before eventually becoming the home of the Luton Museum and Art Gallery in 1931.

Luton Town Council and Committees

The Town Council for the period November 1914 – November 1919 comprised the following members:

NORTH WARD

Aldermen E. Oakley and H. Arnold; Councillors S. Green, J. Unwin, J. H. Hawkes, G. W. Escott, J. Bone and S. B. Hubbard

EAST WARD

Aldermen H. O. Williams and J. H. Staddon; Councillors H. Impey, W. W. Merchant, A. Attwood, A. Chapman, W. A. Rainbow and W. J. Primett.

WEST WARD

Aldermen A. Wilkinson and T. Cain; Councillors G. W. Gilder, G. Warren, C. Dillingham, C. Yarrow, M. Barford and R. F. Biggs

There was one enforced change in June 1917 with the death of Councillor A. A. Oakley. J. H. Hawkes was elected to succeed him by the rest of the Council and not by public election.

COMMITTEES OF THE TOWN COUNCIL — 1919

Peace: Impey*, Arnold, Attwood, Barford, Dillingham, Escott, Oakley, Primett and Yarrow.

Watch: Impey, Arnold, Attwood, Cain, Oakley*, Primett, Staddon and Warren.

Tolls and Municipal Buildings: Impey, Bone, Chapman, Dillingham*, Green, Hawkes, Rainbow, Unwin and Yarrow.

Parks: Impey, Cain, Barford, Bone, Chapman, Gilder, Green, Unwin and Yarrow*.

Notes:

* Denotes Chairman of the Committee.

The Mayor served on all Council Committees. A Committee consisted of nine members. An anomaly to the above was the Watch Committee which had eight members in 1919 but nine in previous years. Impey had served as Chairman of the Parks Committee 1916-1918.

FOOD CONTROL COMMITTEE

Original (Pre Food Strike)

Staddon*, Attwood, Bone, Oakley, Primett, Wilkinson and Yarrow (Council) W. Ball (Co-operative Society) P. Banks (Trades and Labour Council) H. Inwood and W. Saunders (Tradesmen's Association) Mrs Staddon

Reformed (Post Food Strike)

Staddon*, Attwood, Primett, Wilkinson and Yarrow (Council) W. Ball (Co-operative Society) T. Knight, W. Mabley and T. Skelton (Trades and Labour Council) H. Inwood and W Saunders (Tradesmen's Association) Mrs Staddon

* Denotes Chairman of the Committee

WAR TRIBUNAL COMMITTEE

Staddon*, Arnold, Oakley, Primett, Williams (Council) W. Ball and T. Smith (Trades and Labour Council) J. H. Webb and W. R. Phillips (Tradesmen's Associaton) * Denotes Chairman of the Committee

MAYORS OF LUTON 1914-1919

1913-1914 Walter James Primett
1914-1915 Walter James Primett
1915-1916 John Henry Staddon
1916-1917 John Henry Staddon
1917-1918 Charles Dillingham
1918-1919 Henry Impey

The Peace Day Procession
19th July 1919

Chief Marshall – (Chief Constable Charles Griffin) escorted by five mounted police officers).

Tableau – 'Jack Cornwell VC' entered by Charles Strapps.

` Comrades of the Great War' ex-servicemen's contingent.

Float – 'Dominions' entered by Luton Political Clubs.

Friendly Societies contingent.

2nd Volunteer Battalion of the Bedfordshire Regiment Detachment.

Float – 'YMCA' escorted by eight members.

Float – entered by Skefko Ball Bearing Co. Ltd.

Special Constables Detachment (led by Deputy Chief Special Constable Charles Robinson).

Float – entered by Commercial Cars Ltd.

Float – entered by Vauxhall Motors Ltd.

Float – entered by Thermo Electric Ltd.

Float – entered by Davis Gas Stove Co. Ltd.

Land Girls contingent.

Float – entered by George Kent Ltd.

Girl Guides contingent.

Float – entered by Hayward Tyler & Co. Ltd.

Red Cross Society contingent (Wardown VAD Nurses).

Float – ' Peace Enthroned' – Official entry of the Town Council.

Float – 'Child Welfare'.

Float – entered by Luton Tradesman's Association.

Six hundred schoolchildren representing each school in Luton.

The following bands were also in the procession:

Red Cross Silver Prize Band*

Salvation Army No. 1 Band

Salvation Army No. 2 Band

Comrades of the Great War Band

Central Mission Band

*Founded in 1890 the Red Cross Band became one of the country's most successful, winning championships from 1901 to 1923. Subsequently they became the Luton Band.

Luton Borough Police Force July 1919

These officers were all on duty between 19th – 21st July 1919.

GRIFFIN, Charles Chief	Constable
HUNT, Herbert	Inspector
JANES, Frederick	Inspector
DUNCOMBE, Harold	Inspector
SPEIGHT, Charles Warrant	Sergeant
BACON, Arthur Detective	Sergeant
CLARK, Arthur J	Police Sergeant
ANES, Edmund	Police Sergeant
MATSELL, John	Police Sergeant
PARSONS, Henry	Police Sergeant
SMITH, Frederick	Police Sergeant
FROST, Horace	Detective Constable

POLICE CONSTABLES

BILEY, John
HIGHAM, Thomas
BONE, James
HILLS, Henry
BYRON, William
KING, George
CAUSEBROOK, John
KING, Wilfred
CHAPMAN, Arthur
MASON, Thomas
CLEMENTS, Charles
ODELL, Richard
COOPER, Percy
PARSONS, David
ELLINGHAM, Alfred
RHYMES, William
FIELD, Alec
RICHES, David
FIELD, George
ROBERTS, Robert
FOX, Charles
RUSHMER, Robert
FRAMPTON, Robert
SEAR, Albert
FULLER, Arthur
SHAW, Thomas
GARDNER, Sidney
SILVESTER, James
GOSS, Alfred
SIMPKINS, Thomas
GRAVES, Cecil
SKELTON, William
HARPER, Major

STANBRIDGE, George
HEAD, Albert
STEVENS, Harold
HENCHER, Russell
TAYLOR, Herbert
HIGGINS, Albert
WOOD, John
WRIGHT, William

Forty Special Constables were on duty during 19th July commanded by Deputy Special Constable Charles Robinson. Under the Special Constable act of 1914, positions arising from Military service had been filled by Special Constables who were also used to augment the regular force during the war.

Dr William Archibald gave evidence that he treated a total of forty-eight officers, including one from the County force, and ten specials for injuries.

The following officers were detained in the Bute Hospital:

Inspector Hunt :

Injuries to the stomach and head and abrasions to the head. (Hunt was unconscious for much of the night of 19th/20th).

Constable Sear :

Badly cut head and lacerated ear.

(Sear was also semi-conscious for a time)

Constable Taylor :

Severe stomach injuries.

Constable Silvester :

Severe stomach injuries.

Sp. Con. Carter :

Injuries to the head.

The Luton Borough Police Force authorised number of personnel had been set at fifty-two in 1913. This consisted of one Chief Constable; two Inspectors; one Detective Sergeant; one Warrant Sergeant; five Police Sergeants; one Detective Constable and forty-one Police Constables. During 1919, five more Police Constables were added to the strength making a total of fifty-seven.

There was one anomaly in practice. Three inspectors were on the force strength and all were on duty during the riot. Five officers on the strength were still on active service in the armed forces.

The following Police Forces supplied reinforcements:

Bedford Borough Police
St. Ablans City Police
Bedfordshire Constabulary
Hertfordshire Constabulary
Cambridge Borough Police
Northampton Borough Police

The men were billeted at the Court House and the Ceylon Baptist Hall during the week they spent in Luton

Luton Fire Brigade July 1919

The following men attended the fire at the Town Hall, 19th-21st July 1919. The Fire Report logs the first call at 10.25pm (19th July) and the time of leaving the scene at 12.05pm (21st July).

Name : Attendance : Injuries

ANDREW, A., Chief Officer 21 hours

PLUMMER, J. W., Second Officer 18 hours Head, back and body

GEORGE, T., Foreman 30 hours Head

SMITH, D., Foreman 17 hours Legs

BARBER, S. 17 hours Head and back

BATES, H. 18 hours Head(concusion)

BURGESS, W. G.19 hours Head, back and arms

BURGESS, W. 17 hours Head, arm and hands

CLARKE, W. 19 hours Back and side

COOKE, A.17 hours

COWLEY, F. 17 hours Hand, face and arms

DAY, A. 18 hours Right leg and hands

EVANS, G.17 hours

GARRETT, J. 19 hours Shoulder, arm and head

GIDDINGS, S.18 hours Hand, face and arms

IRELAND, G.17 hours Head

IRELAND, N. 17 hours

PEDDAR, W. A. 17 hours Internal injuries

WRIGHT, A. 15 hours

The following civilians received official thanks from the Council for lending assistance to the Fire Brigade:

BURGESS, W. 77 Oak Road

COWLEY, F. 24 Highfield Road

DUMPLETON, Mr Wellington Street

ELLERY, H. W. The Crest' Beech Hill

GARNER, A. 69 Liverpool Road

McCREADY, P. O. 84 Maple Road

MEAD, Private R. 2nd Battalion, Royal Fusiliers

MURPHY, J. 24 Butlin Road

NEAL, J. 152 Ashburnham Road

RUMBALL, F. S. 29 Manchester Street

SAPWELL, H. 114 Ridgeway Road

SAUNDERS, H. 104 Cambridge Street

SHAW, H. Manor Farm, Stopsley

SMITH, G. 59 Edward Street, Dunstable

STANBRIDGE, W. 69 Hastings Street

WELLS, H. S. 54 Reginald Street

WOOD, D. 30 Wimborne Street

THE FIRE BRIGADE — A BRIEF HISTORY TO 1919

A voluntary fire fighting service had existed in Luton from the early nineteenth century and in 1864 it was taken over by the Board of Health and subsequently came under the control of the Corporation in 1876. In 1894 David Teale was appointed Captain of the Fire Brigade, a dual role for him, as he was also the Chief Constable of the Luton Borough Police Force. A purpose-built Fire Station was opened in 1901 on the corner of Church Street and St. Marys Road.

Horse-drawn appliances and voluntary staff were considered adequate for a number of years during the early twentieth century but with expansion, particularly of the engineering factories, the Council decided that a better service needed to be provided. A new motor Fire engine was purchased from Dennis Bros. Ltd. of Guildford at a cost of £998 and was delivered on 30th March 1914. A week earlier, from a short-list of four, Alexander Andrew

had been appointed as motor engineer and driver
with the position of Second Officer. In December
1916 David Teale died and on the 29th Andrew was
appointed to succeed him as the bridgade's first full
time Chief Officer.
June 1918 saw the Fire Brigade become fully
motorised when a second engine was purchased
from Dennis. In 1919 Andrew's complement of
Firemen was eighteen, half of whom were
still volunteers.

THE MOTOR FIRE ENGINES

The motor was driven by a four cylinder, sixty horse
power engine capable of speeds around forty miles
per hour with a full load, including a complement of
eleven men.
Water was supplied by means of a three-stage
Dennis-Gwynne Turbine Pump with a capacity to
deliver between four and five hundred gallons per
minute, at a pressure of up to two hundred pounds
per square inch.
For immediate use at small fires, the motor was
equipped with a First Aid Apparatus. This consisted
of a small auxiliary forty gallon tank, pump and
hose capable of working for four and a half minutes.
Fitted to the motor was a Bayley fifty-two
foot telescopic escape ladder together with
supplementary ladders, two thousand foot of hose,
stand and branch pipes, tools and accessories.
The second motor was identical apart from having
better tyres with improved grip and the First Aid
Apparatus was fed directly from the hydrant instead
of from an auxiliary tank.

The Riot Charges

The Riot Charge will be as follows:

At the Borough of Luton on 19th and 20th July, 1919, together with divers other evil disposed persons to the number of one thousand and more whose names are unknown unlawfully riotously and riotously did assemble and gather together to disturb the public peace and then unlawfully, riotously, and tumultuously did make a great noise riot tumult and disturbance to the great terror and disturbance of His Majesty's subjects there being and residing passing and repassing.

Additional Assault Charge

Then there unlawfully riotously and tumultuously did assault beat wound and ill-treat one . . ., against the Peace of our Sovereign Lord the King his Crown and Dignity.

Charges under the Malicious Damage Act, 1861

At the Borough of Luton on 19th and 20th July, 1919, together with divers other persons to the number of at least one thousand and more whose names are unknown then and there being riotously and tumultuously assembled together to the disturbance of the public peace feloniously did unlawfully and with force destroy a certain building there situate to wit the Town Hall, belonging to the Mayor, Aldermen and Burgesses of the Borough of Luton, contrary to Section 11 of the Malicious Damage Act, 1861.

At the Borough of Luton on 19th and 20th July, 1919, together with divers other persons to the number of at least one thousand and more whose names are unknown then and there being riotously and tumultuously assembled together to the disturbance of the public peace feloniously did unlawfully and with force destroy a certain:

Warehouse there situate of Charles Dillingham

Shop of S. Farmer & Co.

Shop of Walter S. Clark (As the case maybe)

Shop of Charles Casper

Shop of James Neve Brown Ltd.

Building there situate belonging to the Borough of Luton, contrary to Section 12 of the Malicious Damage Act, 1861.

The Defendants

The following twenty-seven men and one woman were sent for trial at Bedford Assizes, 17th-24th October 1919.

ARTHUR BARRETT.

Address: 48 North Street
Age: 58. Occupation: Labourer.
MILITARY SERVICE: Two years' service in the army.
CRIMINAL RECORD: No previous convictions. Police Sergeant Smith stated at the trial that he had known Barrett for twenty years and considered him a law abiding citizen. Prior to the war Barrett had worked for the Council for eighteen years.

CHARGE: RIOTING

The prosecution alleged that Barrett made a speech that incited the crowd and that he made persistent efforts to get into the Town Hall in the afternoon. In his defence Barrett did not deny making a speech but that he only expressed grievances about his treatment in the army and aired his views about Luton Corporation.

SENTENCE: ACQUITTED

(Judge Greer stated that in his view the case amounted to nothing more than a good-natured grouse expressed in rather strong language on a very unfortunate occasion.)

WILLIAM BATTAMS.

Address: 51 Hartley Road
Age: 48. Occupation: Labourer
MILITARY SERVICE: Joined the Royal Flying Corps in July 1917 as an Air Mechanic. After training he was sent to France where he was stationed at Boulogne in RFC repair shops. Awarded the General Service and Victory Medals.
CRIMINAL RECORD: No previous convictions. He was described at the trial as a law abiding citizen and had been a tenant of Henry Impey for fifteen years who Battams said had been a gentleman to him.

CHARGE: RIOTING AND DEMOLITION

The prosecution alleged that Battams incited the crowd in front of the Town Hall between 6-6.30pm and that he was under the influence of drink. He was accompanied by Joseph Pursey.
In his defence Battams did not deny making a speech at the time stated but said that at this time there was no riot in progress.

SENTENCE: ACQUITTED

GEORGE BODSWORTH.

Address: 12 Burr Street
Age: 35. Occupation: Painter
MILITARY SERVICE: Had served in the 1st Rifle Brigade until 1906. Called up as a reservist on the outbreak of war and joined the 3rd Rifle Brigade. Served in the retreat at Mons where he was wounded and was discharged after two years' service with an army pension.
CRIMINAL RECORD: Previous convictions for Stealing, Assault and being Drunk and Disorderly.

CHARGE: RIOTING, DEMOLITION AND ASSAULT

The prosecution alleged that Bodsworth was in front of the Town Hall between 11.00pm and 1.00am. During the police charges he was seen shouting and waving a stick at the bottom of Wellington Street and at one point rushed from the crowd and hit a police officer in the chest.

In his defence Bodsworth said that he was struck on the head and knocked unconscious and did not hit any police officer. When he regained consciousness he was at home.

SENTENCE: GUILTY: RIOTING AND ASSAULT
ACQUITTED: DEMOLITION 3 MONTHS' IMPRISONMENT

(Judge Greer stated 'I do not think you are a really bad fellow but it is very serious to get violent on these occasions.')

HARRY BOWLES.

Address: 56 Tavistock Street
Age: 34. Occupation: Labourer
MILITARY SERVICE: Volunteered in December 1914 as Private in 10th Hampshire Regiment. Sent to Egypt in 1915. Also served on the Vardar Front in Salonika and in 1918 in Russia. Demobilised in April 1919. Awarded the 1914-15 Star and General Service Medals.
CRIMINAL RECORD: No previous convictions. He was described at the trial as a man of previous good character.

CHARGE: RIOTING

The prosecution alleged that Bowles was seen urging on various speakers, Gore in particular, in front of the Town Hall in the afternoon.

In his defence Bowles said that all he had done was to shout at Gore to speak up.

SENTENCE: ACQUITTED

(Judge Greer stated there was room for doubt as to whether Bowles took any part in the riot and advised him to keep out of such crowds in the future.)

GEORGE BUGGS.

Address: 52 North Street
Age: 25. Occupation: Boxmaker
MILITARY SERVICE: Unknown
CRIMINAL RECORD: No previous convictions. At the trial a witness gave him an excellent character reference.

CHARGE: RIOTING AND DEMOLITION

The prosecution alleged that Buggs was seen in Farmers music shop. After the pianos had been taken out into the street he was heard to say 'now for the safe'.

In his defence Buggs said that he was never in Farmers music shop or any other shop and it was a case of mistaken identity. He admitted to watching the fire at the Town Hall for about forty-five minutes.

SENTENCE: ACQUITTED

(Judge Greer stated that he had received the benefit of the doubt.)

CHARLES COPLEY.

Address: 5 Langley Place
Age: 37. Occupation: Rag Collector
MILITARY SERVICE: Unknown
CRIMINAL RECORD: Unknown
CHARGE: RIOTING, DEMOLITION AND ASSAULT
The prosecution alleged that Copley incited the crowd in front of the Town Hall in the afternoon. He was together with Barrett, Gore and Kempson. When the rush into the Town Hall was made he was one of the first into the building.

In his defence Copley said that he went to the Town Hall in the afternoon to look for a friend, Kempson, with whom he had been earlier. Miles was speaking but he could not hear what was being said. He could not find Kempson so he went home.

SENTENCE: GUILTY: RIOTING
ACQUITTED: DEMOLITION AND ASSAULT
3 MONTHS IMPRISONMENT

FREDERICK WILLIAM COULDRIDGE.

Address: 1 Buxton Road
Age: 38. Occupation: Watchman
MILITARY SERVICE: Enlisted in August 1914 in the Bedfordshire Regiment. Appointed Stretcher Bearer. Saw action at the battles of the Somme and Arras. Was wounded twice and was invalided home with a heart condition before being discharged on July 2nd 1917.
CRIMINAL RECORD: No previous convictions.

CHARGE: RIOTING, DEMOLITION AND ASSAULT

The prosecution alleged that Couldridge was inciting the crowd in front of the Town Hall during the evening. He was also seen in the doorway of Dillingham's hat factory in Upper George Street from where he was urging the crowd to rush the firemen and police. From here it was alleged he had thrown a lump of iron at Chief Officer Andrew which struck him on the helmet.

In his defence Couldridge denied all the charges and said that he was at the Town Hall with friends about 10.30pm. He then left them for a time but took no part in the rioting. He was near Williamson Street for part of the time and did not see a single policeman, fireman or engine. At about midnight he went home.

SENTENCE: GUILTY: RIOTING AND ASSAULT
ACQUITTED: DEMOLITION
18 MONTHS IMPRISONMENT

WITHOUT HARD LABOUR

(Couldridge asked if the Judge would deal with him leniently as he was disabled and receiving a pension. Judge Greer replied that he could not. He said that Couldridge was a man of education and great intelligence and ` when a man like you takes part in proceedings of this sort what can be expected of ignorant labourers and boys?')

WILLIAM DIXON.

Address: 47 Hartley Road
Age: 43. Occupation: Boiler Maker
MILITARY SERVICE: Unknown
CRIMINAL RECORD: No previous convictions. At the trial he was given an excellent character reference by his employer.

CHARGE: RIOTING, DEMOLITION AND ASSAULT

The prosecution alleged that Dixon was seen throwing missiles at the Town Hall windows between 12.00pm and 1.00am. During the police charge he struck a policeman over the eye with a stick before being knocked down by the policeman. Later he was seen in the Town Hall where he was knocked down. In his defence Dixon said that he went out in the evening and drunk some whiskey for the first time in nine years. He then went to see what was going on at the Town Hall and as soon as he got in the crowd he was knocked down. He was unconscious for a time and came to in the Town Hall where a policeman was bathing his head. He believed he had been pushed through a window of the Town Hall. Dixon admitted to being drunk.

SENTENCE: GUILTY OF ALL CHARGES 9 MONTHS IN SECOND DIVISION

(Judge Greer stated that it was with deep regret that he had to pass such a severe sentence.)

STANLEY DOLBY.

Address: 8 Adelaide Terrace
Age: 25. Occupation: Unknown
MILITARY SERVICE: Enlisted in 1914 and sent to France. Was wounded on five separate occasions before being discharged in 1918.
CRIMINAL RECORD: No previous convictions. At the trial Inspector Janes stated he had known Dolby since childhood.

CHARGE: RIOTING, DEMOLITION AND ASSAULT

The prosecution alleged that Dolby was seen in the Town Clerk's office with Smith where a small fire had been started. He was struck by a police officer before being ejected.

In his defence Dolby said he spent the evening in a public house and went home at 10.00pm. He had supper and went to bed about 10.45pm. He denied absolutely being at the Town Hall.

SENTENCE: GUILTY: RIOTING ACQUITTED: DEMOLITION AND ASSAULT 9 MONTHS IMPRISONMENT

GEORGE FOWLER.

Address: 6 Albert Terrace
Age: 21. Occupation: Carter
MILITARY SERVICE: Unknown
CRIMINAL RECORD: Thirteen previous convictions including wilful damage, assaults on the police and stealing. For the last offence he had received two months' hard labour in May 1919.
CHARGE: RIOTING, DEMOLITION AND ASSAULT
The prosecution alleged that Fowler was involved in the afternoon disturbance outside the Mayor's home. About 10.30pm it was also alleged that he pulled a policeman to the ground outside the Town Hall and kicked him before being struck by another officer. Later on in the evening he was ejected from the Town Clerk's office. In his defence Fowler denied all the charges.

SENTENCE: GUILTY: RIOTING AND ASSAULT ACQUITTED: DEMOLITION 15 MONTH HARD LABOUR

(Fowler asked the Judge to take into account the fact that he had served thirteen weeks in custody and Judge Greer's original sentence of eighteen months was reduced by three months.)

JOHN HENRY GOOD.

Address: 74 Dane Road
Age: 46. Occupation: Labourer
MILITARY SERVICE: Unknown
CRIMINAL RECORD: No previous convictions
CHARGE: RIOTING AND DEMOLITION
The prosecution alleged that Good was one of the leaders who rushed the Town Hall in the afternoon. He was also seen inciting the crowd in front of the Town Hall at about 1.00am.

In his defence Good said that he had been asked by the Comrades to take part in the procession. He had declined as he found it difficult to march having suffered two accidents in France on active service. He watched the procession from the bottom of Wellington Street and there was some noise but he denied doing anything to incite the crowd. He agreed that he went to the Town Hall after watching the fireworks display but went home around midnight.

SENTENCE: GUILTY: RIOTING ACQUITTED: DEMOLITON 2 MONTHS IMPRISONMENT

Judge Greer said he took into account the fact that the prisoner used no obscene language.)

GEORGE GOODSHIP.
Address: 129 Highbury Road.
Age: 42. Occupation: Fitter
MILITARY SERVICE: Had served in the Navy for twenty-seven years. Awarded the China and South African Medals and the General Service and Victory Medals.
CRIMINAL RECORD: No previous convictions.
The prosecution alleged that Goodship was in front of the Two Hall in the afternoon and was inciting the crowd to fetch out the Mayor and Town Clerk. He was also one of the leaders in the rush into the Town Hall. In his defence Goodship admitted he was on the Town Hall steps in the afternoon but did not take part in the rush. Later he was carried forward by the crowd and forced to the side where he gave assistance to a disabled soldier. When the chairs were thrown out of the assembly room he went inside to implore the people not to throw them out because of the danger to the women and children. He also contended it was a case of mistaken identity as P. S. Smith had originally identified another man when he came to arrest Goodship at Laportes where he worked. Two witnesses gave evidence on his behalf.

SENTENCE: GUILTY: RIOTING ACQUITTED: DEMOLITION 3 MONTHS IMPRISONMENT
(Judge Greer admitted the case over the identification was unsatisfactory but was of little importance as the prisoner admitted he was there.)

EPHRAIM GORE.
Address: 35 Windsor Street.
Age: 45. Occupation: Iron Erector
MILITARY SERVICE: Served with the 2nd Bedfordshire Regiment between 1891-1904. Re-enlisted August 5th with the Bedford's and served overseas. Discharged in 1915. Re-enlisted again in the Royal Engineers and served for another year with 10 months overseas before being discharged with a pension.
CRIMINAL RECORD: Forty-one previous convictions including larceny, vagrancy, wilful damage, assault, obscene language, poaching, fighting and refusing to leave licensed premises. Twice sent to reformatory and other sentences included seven and twenty-one days, one, two and four months and in May 1913 he was given a sentence of nine months at Bedford Assizes. At the trial Inspector Janes said he had known Gore for too long to have been mistaken about his identity.

CHARGE: RIOTING AND DEMOLITION
The prosecution alleged that Gore made a speech in front of the Town Hall in the afternoon, although it was more moderate than others that were made. He was also seen to pull down the electric illuminations that were hanging from the building and to have struck a match and set fire to the flags and decorations that had been torn down.
In his defence Gore said he was going to go to Wardown and stopped at the Town Hall about 3.30pm and listened to a couple of speeches. He then got onto the Town Hall parapet and made a speech but it was only about his pension and the Workhouse. He denied setting fire to the decorations.

SENTENCE: GUILTY: RIOTING ACQUITTED: DEMOLITION 9 MONTHS IMPRISONMENT
(Judge Greer said that the burning of flags did not justify a charge of damaging the Town Hall but was evidence of participation in the riot. Originally the

sentence was nine months hard labour but on a plea from Gore that he would lose his pension the Judge amended it. Gore expressed his thanks.)

GEORGE HELEY.

Address: 25 Gloucester Road
Age: 22.Occupation: Sailor
MILITARY SERVICE: He had served in the Navy since 1913 and had been wounded twice.
CRIMINAL RECORD: No previous convictions.

CHARGE: RIOTING, DEMOLITION AND ASSAULT

The prosecution alleged that Heley was among those who tried to rush the Town Hall about 10.15pm. It was alleged that he was heard to threaten to `kill' a policeman and to then have hit an officer on the jaw, another in the stomach and to have kicked a third officer. He was seen several times through the evening inciting the crowd and was easily identifiable owing to the fact he was wearing his naval uniform.

In his defence Heley said that in the evening he found himself in a large crowd at the Town Hall. Something hit him a severe blow on the back of the head and then events were muddled and he did not know what happened until 3.30am when he went home. He admitted to having a drink earlier in the evening but did not remember trying to get up the Town Hall steps or striking any policemen.

SENTENCE: GUILTY: RIOTING AND ASSAULT
ACQUITTED: DEMOLITION
12 MONTHS IMPRISONMENT

(Judge Greer said he was very sorry to see a man in navy uniform in the dock. On the evening in question the prisoner was particularly violent. He would have imposed a term of penal servitude but for his good military service and age.)

CHARLES KEEN.

Address: 73 Highbury Road
Age: 40. Occupation: Blocker
MILITARY SERVICE: Enlisted as a private in the Royal Warwickshire Regiment in November 1916. Drafted to India in July 1917 and was on garrison duty at Poona, Rawal Pindi and Bangalore. Returned to England after eighteen months service and demobbed in March 1919. Awarded the General Service and Victory Medals.
CRIMINAL RECORD: No previous convictions.

CHARGE: RIOTING, DEMOLITION AND ASSAULT

The prosecution alleged that Keen had been seen throwing missiles at the firemen for about an hour. He had used stones, wood, iron and even broken glass from the shattered Town Hall windows. In the process he had struck Chief Officer Andrew and knocked one of his firemen unconscious.

In his defence Keen said that he went with his wife to look at the decorations and illuminations and got to the Town Hall just before 10.00pm. There was a large crowd and his wife wanted to stay and watch. They stood near the library steps and then moved towards Wellington Street at about 1.00am. There a fireman was turning a hose on the crowd but he did not throw missiles at the fireman. A little later they went home. His wife gave evidence that they were together the whole time and said that she had persuaded her husband to stay.

SENTENCE: ACQUITTED

ERNEST KEMPSON.

Address: New Town Street
Age: Unknown. Occupation: Unknown
MILITARY SERVICE: He joined the army in January

1918 but was discharged as medically unfit in December 1918 without having served overseas.

CRIMINAL RECORD: Twenty-nine previous convictions including poaching, assault, wilful damage, gaming, street betting, threats, obscene language and being drunk and disorderly. At Bedford Assizes in June 1912 he was sentenced to five years Penal Servitude for rape.

CHARGE: RIOTING

The prosecution alleged that Kempson made a speech outside the Town Hall in the afternoon in which he used obscene language. He also cheered the speeches of Gore and Miles when they were inciting the crowd and took part in the disturbance outside the Mayor's house.

In his defence Kempson said he heard a lot of cheering at the Town Hall and went to see what was going on. He listened to a speech by Gore and then went with the crowd to the Mayor's hours. In the evening he went out again but denied inciting the crowd although he agreed he could get a bit excitable.

SENTENCE: GUILTY: RIOTING
6 MONTHS HARD LABOUR

(Judge Greer said it was fortunate that Kempson was not connected with the more serious rioting as he had a very bad record.)

MAUD KITCHENER.

Address: Gaitskill Row
Age: 40. Occupation: Machinist
MILITARY SERVICE: None
CRIMINAL RECORD: Previous convictions for assault, fighting, obscene language and disorderly behaviour.

CHARGE: RIOTING,
DEMOLITION AND ASSAULT

The prosecution alleged that Kitchener was on the Manchester Street side of the Town Hall between 11.00 and 12.00pm. She was inciting the crowd to attack the police and was using obscene language. She was easily identifiable as she was wearing a soldier's tunic and cap.

In her defence Kitchener pleaded that she had no intention of inciting anyone.

SENTENCE: GUILTY: RIOTING
ACQUITTED: DEMOLITION
AND ASSAULT
6 MONTHS IMPRISONMENT

(Judge Greer said that he could not pass over this offence. 'You are known to be a dangerous character and difficult for the police.')

CHARLES LAMBERT.

Address: 37 Stanley Street
Age: 63. Occupation: Blocker
MILITARY SERVICE: Unknown
CRIMINAL RECORD: Unknown
CHARGE: RIOTING AND ASSAULT

The prosecution alleged that Lambert struck P. C. Higham in the face during the baton charge towards Wellington Street. He was also under the influence of drink. In his defence Lambert said he got to the Town Hall shortly after10.00pm. He was then assisting some women to get away from the danger from the police baton charge and was knocked down. He did not hit a policeman. He got out of the crowd, went to check the warehouse where he worked was not damaged and then went home.

SENTENCE: GUILTY: RIOTING
AND ASSAULT
BOUND OVER

(Judge Greer accepted his explanation with drink inside him he had got irritated when pushed about.)

JOHN STANLEY LONG.

Address: 19 Alma Street
Age: 40. Occupation: Labourer
MILITARY SERVICE: Served in the Hussars between 1893-1903. Was wounded in 1899 during the Boer War. Enlisted in the Yeomanry on 11th September 1914 before being invalided out on medical grounds in October 1916 without serving overseas.
CRIMINAL RECORD: Thirty-six convictions including wilful damage, vagrancy, drunk and disorderly, obscene language, assault on police officers, fighting and larceny. Was sentenced at various times to six, ten and eighteen months and spent three years in a reformatory. While serving in the Hussars he was court marshalled and given six months hard labour before being discharged. (Presumably he was allowed to re-enlist with the outbreak of the Boer War in 1899.)

CHARGE: RIOTING AND DEMOLITION

The prosecution alleged that Long was one of the leaders who were in the Town Hall in the afternoon. During the evening he was seen during the police baton charges behaving in a noisy and violent manner. In his defence Long said that after the procession had passed the bottom of Alma Street he and his sister went to the Town Hall. It had been entered and they both went in. He agreed he was at the Town Hall in the evening but saw no baton charges.

SENTENCE: GUILTY: RIOTING ACQUITTED: DEMOLITION 18 MONTHS HARD LABOUR

(Judge Greer described this as one of the more serious cases.)

ROBERT MARSHALL.

Address: 12 Butlin Road
Age: 18. Occupation: Moulder
MILITARY SERVICE: None.
CRIMINAL RECORD: No previous convictions.

CHARGE: RIOTING, DEMOLITION AND ASSAULT

The prosecution alleged that Marshall was in the vicinity of Dillingham's warehouse in Upper George Street throwing bricks and stones at the firemen through the evening.
In his defence Marshall gave a most emphatic denial to all the charges and claimed to have been assisting the firemen. In this he was supported by his employer who gave evidence that Marshall helped him in using a hose and he had sent in his name as a helper.

SENTENCE: ACQUITTED

(Judge Greer said that Chief Officer Andrew was kept very busy and he could have made a mistake in identification. The Judge could not help but be impressed with Marshall's demeanour in the witness box and he had struck him as someone who was describing the events rather than inventing a story.)

HENRY WILLIAM (HARRY) MILES.

Address: 7 Gloucester Road
Age: 38. Occupation: Cinema Operator
MILITARY SERVICE: At the battle of St. Julien, Private Miles volunteered to go through heavy shell fire to obtain aid. He was successful but was wounded in the process. For his action he was awarded the Military Medal which was presented to him by Mayor Henry Impey.
CRIMINAL RECORD: No previous convictions.

CHARGE: RIOTING AND DEMOLITION

The prosecution alleged that Miles made a speech in front of the Town Hall in the afternoon inciting the crowd. He referred to himself as a revolutionary and a Bolshevist and also offered to lead the crowd to the Mayor's House.

In his defence Miles' counsel made an impassioned plea that the two minutes of incoherent nonsense' in which Miles indulged was that of someone who had become so excited that he might have said anything. It was exactly what happened with someone suffering from shell shock who had lost their head completely. Miles in his defence denied using the word Bolshevist.

SENTENCE: GUILTY: RIOTING
ACQUITTED: DEMOLITION
BOUND OVER

(Judge Greer stated that whether or not the word Bolshevist was used, Miles probably did not really understand its meaning and had no intention of urging the crowd to become Bolshevists. That, however was not the point. He was a man of undoubted respectability who had used inflammatory words and it was dangerous to suggest that he did not know what he was doing. Although his involvement was to some extent accidental and unintentional, Miles was still part of the events.)

WILFRED HAROLD OVENALL.

Address: 73a Ashburnham Road
Age: 34. Occupation: Schoolmaster
MILITARY SERVICE: Enlisted in the R.A.M.C. and then transferred to the Royal Fusiliers in 1915 with whom he was granted a commission. He suffered severe shell shock at the battle of Arras in 1917 and was discharged as medically unfit in May 1918.
CRIMINAL RECORD: No previous convictions.
CHARGE: RIOTING AND

DEMOLITION

The prosecution alleged that Ovenall was standing in the entrance to Dillingham's warehouse in Upper George Street from where he was throwing missiles at the firemen between 1.00 and 2.00am.

In his defence Ovenall said that on the night of the riot he did not get back from London until nearly 1.00am and was then making his way home. When he got to Upper George Street he was deluged with water from a hose and he got into a doorway, cut his hand and remembered nothing further.

SENTENCE: ACQUITTED

(Ovenall had been awarded a MA Degree with double honours at Oxford. At the time of the riot he was still appearing before Luton medical boards with nerve trouble. He held the position of Classics master at Luton Modern School.)

FREDERICK PLATER.

Address: 69 Chase Street
Age: 27. Occupation: Labourer
MILITARY SERVICE: Served for nearly four years in the army including overseas in France and Salonika.
CRIMINAL RECORD: No previous convictions.
CHARGE: RIOTING, DEMOLITION, ASSAULT AND THEFT

The prosecution alleged that Plater during the evening climbed onto a fire engine in the charge of Chief Officer Andrew and removed one of the hoses. Later on he was seen to strike Second Officer Plummer with either a stick or a truncheon and then punch him as he fell. At about 1.00am he was involved in smashing the windows of Brown's boot and shoe shop from where he took goods. All the allegations took part in Manchester Street and Plater was easily identifiable as he was dressed in a cleric's clothes.

In his defence Plater said that he put on the clerical clothes and then went for a drink at two public houses. Then he went to his mother's house and changed leaving the clerical clothes there. He then went to Wardown and left about 10.40pm and got home about 4.00am. Questioned about the long time gap he said he only stood in the crowd and that was all he remembered. Everything said against him was false and he denied it all.

SENTENCE: GUILTY: RIOT, ASSAULT AND THEFT
ACQUITTED: DEMOLITION
3 YEARS PENAL SERVITUDE

(Judge Greer said that this was the most serious of all the cases. Plater took advantage of the serious rioting to commit a series of very serious offences.)

JOSEPH FREDERICK PURSEY.

Address: 14 Midland Road
Age: 26. Occupation: Attendant
MILITARY SERVICE: Enlisted in the Leicestershire Regiment in 1914 and served until he was demobilised in March 1919 during which time he was wounded three times.
CRIMINAL RECORD: No previous convictions. At the trial it was stated that he 'bore good character'.

CHARGE: RIOTING AND DEMOLITION

The prosecution alleged that Pursey stood on the Town Hall steps during the afternoon counting down the minutes and urging the crowd to fetch the Mayor out. This was after the Town Hall had been rushed. He was also seen to climb a lamppost and try to pull off the top and was one of those who tried to get into the Town Hall about 5.30pm. Pursey was also alleged to have taken part in the disturbance outside the Mayor's home in the afternoon.
In his defence Pursey said that he watched the procession from Cheapside and then went to see what was going on at the Town Hall. He pushed to the front of the crowd and then gave a speech about how he had been treated in the army. He denied counting down the minutes or that he had clung to a lamppost to pull off the top but admitted going to the Mayor's house.

SENTENCE: GUILTY: RIOTING
ACQUITTED: DEMOLITION
3 MONTHS IMPRISONMENT

SIDNEY GEORGE QUINCE.

Address: 66 Hitchin Road.
Age: 29. Occupation: Labourer
MILITARY SERVICE: Enlisted in the army in November 1914 but discharged in the December. (Quince must have previously served in the army as a regular soldier as he was twice charged with desertion in 1908)
CRIMINAL RECORD: Twice bound over for assault.

CHARGE: RIOTING

The prosecution alleged that Quince was in front of the Town Hall during the afternoon. When the Town Hall was rushed he was one of the first into the building. Later in the afternoon he was inciting the crowd to fetch out the Mayor and was with Miles when he made his speech.
In his defence Quince admitted being at the Town Hall in the afternoon but said that he was deaf and out of curiosity made a push forward to hear what was being said. A minute or two later a rush was made up the Town Hall steps and those who were in the front were forced into the building.

SENTENCE: GUILTY: RIOTING
4 MONTHS HARD LABOUR

(Judge Greer said that the prisoner had a very bad record and should get out of his bad ways.)

JAMES ROBINSON.

Address: 3 New Street

Age: 45. Occupation: Labourer

MILITARY SERVICE: He enlisted in 1914 with the Royal Engineers as a Sapper. Drafted to France, he served in the retreat from Mons and at Armentieres. He was discharged in December 1915 due to his service. Awarded the Mons Star, General Service and Victory Medals.

CRIMINAL RECORD: No previous convictions. At the trial he was described as a man of good character.

CHARGE: RIOTING AND DEMOLITION

The prosecution alleged that Robinson was inciting the crowd in front of the Town Hall in the afternoon and was one of those who was ejected from the building by the police. He was also involved in the disturbance at the Mayor's home where he attempted to climb over the railings.

In his defence Robinson said that he was in New Bedford Road when the procession passed by and he then made his way to the Town Hall. A lot of people were going into the building and out of curiosity he followed them in as he thought he had a right to enter a public building. He denied he went to the Mayor's house.

SENTENCE: ACQUITTED

ALBERT SMITH.

Address: Adelaide Terrace

Age: 35. Occupation: Labourer

MILITARY SERVICE: Served for nearly four years in the army during which time he was wounded.

CRIMINAL RECORD: Fifteen previous convictions.

CHARGE: RIOTING, DEMOLITION AND ASSAULT

The prosecution alleged that Smith was at the Town Hall about 4.00pm with Fowler. He was wearing a Union Jack in place of a cap and appeared to be drunk. Later in the afternoon about 5.30pm he tried to get into the Town Hall. About 1.00am he was seen throwing bottles and missiles at the Town Hall. In his defence Smith said that he stopped outside the Town Hall in the afternoon as there were too many people to try to get past to go home. He heard some speeches and booing before he moved on about 6.00pm and spent th evening at a public house until 10.00pm. He agreed that he was at the Town Hall shortly after and was then hit on the head by an unknown person. Smith denied he was drunk.

SENTENCE: GUILTY: RIOTING AND ASSAULT
ACQUITTED: DEMOLITION
15 MONTHS HARD LABOUR

WILLIAM TROTT.

Address: 73 Ashton Road

Age: 34. Occupation: Labourer

MILITARY SERVICE: Unknown

CRIMINAL RECORD: Unknown

CHARGE: RIOTING AND DEMOLITION

The prosecution alleged that Trott was seen to strike windows of the Town Hall on the Upper George Street side during the evening.

In his defence Trott said that he had difficulty controlling his arm due to a nervous condition he suffered from.

SENTENCE: ACQUITTED

DEFINITION OF SENTENCES
HARD LABOUR — the penalty of compulsory physical labour imposed in addition to a sentence of imprisonment. Abolished 1948.
PENAL SERVITUDE — the imprisonment of an offender and his subjection to hard labour. It was substituted for transportation in 1853 and abolished 1948.

BEDFORD ASSIZES — DEFENCE COUNSEL

Mr H. B. DRYSDALE WOODCOCK represented Battams, Buggs and Dixon. Sir RYLAND ADKINS MP represented Barrett and Lambert. Mr C. E. DYER KC assisted by Mr B. CAMPION represented Marshall and Ovenall. Mr J. P. STIMSON represented for Robinson. (They were instructed by Mr H. W. LATHOM.)

Sir RYLAND ADKINS MP represented Bodsworth and Miles. Mr B. CAMPION and Captain LOSEBY MP represented Good, Goodship, Heley and Long. Mr J. P. STIMSON represented Bowles, Dolby, Gore and Keen. (They were instructed by Mr C. BARBER.) Copley, Couldridge, Fowler, Kempson, Kitchener, Plater, Pursey, Quince, Smith and Trott were not defended.

The following men and women appeared at Luton Borough Court only and were charged with Larceny:

ADA ANDREWS.

Address: 45 Cobden Street
Age: 23. Occupation: Housewife
CHARGE: Stealing a quantity of toilet requisites value £1.12.6d.
SENTENCE: Fined 40 shillings or fourteen days.

ROSE WINIFRED BACON.

Address: 28 New Street
Age: 21. Occupation: Unknown
CHARGE: Stealing a bottle of scent and two books value 1016d.
SENTENCE: Fined 25 shillings or ten days in each case.

BERTHA FIELD.

Address: 39 Duke Street
Age: 47. Occupation: Machinist

CHARGE: Stealing two boxes of face wax, one bottle and one book.
SENTENCE: Fined 40 shillings or fourteen days.

ELLEN GILBERT.

Address: 3 New Street Age: 37.
Occupation: Machinist
CHARGE: Receipt of toilet requisites stolen by Amos Gooch.
SENTENCE: Fined £3 or twenty-one days.

EMILY GILBERT (daughter of above).

Address: 11 New Street
Age: 19. Occupation: Machinist
CHARGE: Stealing an umbrella value 10/6d.
SENTENCE: Fined 40 shillings or fourteen days.

AMOS GOOCH.

Address: 22 St. Anns Road
Age: 38. Occupation: Blocker
CHARGE: Stealing toilet requisites value 4/3d.
SENTENCE: Fined £5 or one month and was bound over for twelve months.

EDGAR CECIL GOODRIDGE.

Address: 63 Collingdon Street
Age: 39. Occupation: Electrician
CHARGE: Stealing a gramophone value £8.8s.
SENTENCE: £5 or one month.

ELLEN LOUISE GOODRIDGE (wife of above).

Address: 63 Collingdon Street
Age: 34. Occupation: Cleaner
CHARGE: Stealing a gramophone value £8.8s.
SENTENCE: £5 or one month.

EMILY TILCOCK.

Address: 3 New Street Age: 49. Occupation:
Straw Hat Worker CHARGE: Stealing 3 odd
slippers value 7/6d.
SENTENCE: Fined 30 shillings or 30 days.

WALTER WELLS.

Address: 15 Mill Street
Age: 52. Occupation: Labourer
CHARGE: Stealing one pair of boots value £1.8s.6d.
SENTENCE: Fined £5 and ordered to pay £1.8s.6d for
the boots and fifteen shillings Court costs.
The charges against the following man were
withdrawn by the Town Clerk:

GEORGE SAUNDERS.

Address: 23 York Street
Age: 30. Occupation: Labourer
CHARGE: Rioting and Demolition
SENTENCE: Bound over in the sum of £10 to keep
the peace for twelve months.

LUTON BOROUGH COURT —
DEFENCE COUNSEL

Mr H. W. LATHOM represented Andrews, Barrett,
Battams, Bowles, Buggs, Couldridge, Dixon, Field,
Fowler, Goodridge Edgar, Goodridge Ellen, Goodship,
Kitchener, Lambert, Marshall, Ovenall, Pursey,
Robinson, Tilcock and Wells.
Mr C. BARBER represented Bodsworth, Copley, Gooch,
Good, Gore, Heley, Keen, Long, Miles and Plater.
Bacon, Dolby, Gilbert Ellen, Gilbert Emily, Kempson,
Quince, Saunders, Smith and Trott were
not defended.

Riot Odds and Ends

The Riot Act — A statute of 1715 by which persons committing a riot had to disperse within an hour of the reading of the act by a magistrate.

During the afternoon of Peace Day the police on duty in the town centre were wearing their Straw Helmets, unique to the Luton force.

A civilian apparently wanting to assist the police in their baton charges, was seen to line up with them, brandishing a walking stick. Unfortunately for him his motives were mistaken and he received a whack on the head from a truncheon for his trouble.

The story has passed down over the years that the Town Hall clock struck midnight, then crashed down to the ground to cheers from the crowd. The tale is certainly apocryphal. The Town Hall was evacuated by most of the police officers at about 12.20pm. Griffin, Smith and Rignall put the time they left around 12.40pm and the *Luton Reporter* of Tuesday 21st carried an item that the last time the hands were seen they were at 12.30pm.

The key to the front door of the Town Hall was salvaged from the ruins and remained in private hands for over fifty years. It was returned anonymously to the office of the *Evening Post* in 1975 when the now defunct newspaper ran a serialisation of the book *'A View from the Alley'*. On 21st May 1975 the key was presented to the Mayor of Luton, Councillor Des Fuller, and is now on display at Luton Museum.

Numerals from the Town Hall clock face can be seen on display at Luton Museum together with the Penfold hexagonal pillar box that stood outside the Town Hall (see photographs) and now stands outside the Museum entrance.

When the Town Hall ruins were pulled down a number of bricks were stored by the Corporation Housing Department for future use. Unfortunately there is no record of where they were eventually used.

Trouble broke out in Liverpool and Birkenhead in the first week of August when the police force went on strike. The threat that was overheard, that 'Another Luton job' would be carried out on the Birkenhead Town Hall did not materialise after the Military authorities took control of the situation.

There was one unfortunate consequence of the riot for some Lutonians who were due to go on holiday in the late summer. Seaside landladies, obviously aware of the trouble that had occurred and concerned about who their guests might be, cancelled a number of bookings.

In the middle of a submission by Sir Ryland Adkins at Bedford Assizes, the foreman of the Jury was seen to shake his head. Assuming the movement was an indication of dissent Adkins turned to him and said 'But I say yes, I have it in evidence'. Laughter greeted the foreman's explanation that the gesture had been caused by a fly that had been irritating him.

A moment of light relief was provided at Bedford Assizes when, after being sentenced to three months in prison, George Bodsworth wished Judge Greer a

'Merry Christmas and Happy New Year'.
'You just try and keep quiet,' advised the Judge.
'I will Sir. I'll see that they don't catch me anymore,'
replied Bodsworth, causing a roar of laughter in the
courtroom.

The biggest air raid over Luton in the Second World
War claimed the life of Harry Miles, who had won
the Military Medal in the Great War. On the 30th
August 1940 one hundred and ninety-four bombs
were dropped on the South of the town claiming
fifty-nine lives. A single one thousand kilo bomb hit
the Corporation Bus Dept in Park Street. Miles was
the only fatality. At the time he was still living at 7
Gloucester Road.

The number of claims for compensation was
fifty-four.

A total of £3,100.15s.7d was claimed and
£2,137.11s.9d paid out.

The highest claim, £875.4s.3d, was submitted
by W. S. Clark of George Street who were paid
£726.10s.0d. This was for damage to premises,
fixtures and fittings, damaged and stolen stock and
loss of profits.

The lowest claim was for 10s.0d submitted by W. A.
Newbury of the Engineer's Department of the Town
Council for lost money which was paid.
The estimate for the Borough Rate for 1920,
payable from 1st April, increased from £15,231 to
£28,202 and the General District Rate from £20,140
to £27,122 due to the cost of the riot.
The Town Hall was not insured.

BIBLIOGRAPHY

Published Sources
General Books

Bourne, J. M. *Britain and the Great War 1914- 191 8.* (Edward Arnold. 1994)

Douglas, Roy. *History of the Liberal Party 1 895-1970.* (Sidgwick & Jackson. 1971)

Marwick, Arthur. *The Deluge (British Society and the First World War).*
(The Bodley Head Ltd. 1965)

Reese, Peter. *Homecoming Heroes.* (Leo Cooper. 1992)

Stevenson, John. *British Society 1914-45 .* (Pelican. 1984)

Webster, F. A. M. *The History of the Fifth Battalion* (Captain) *The Bedfordshire and
Hertfordshire Regiment (T.A.).* (Frederick Warne & Co. Ltd. 1930)

Winter, Denis. *Deaths Men — Soldiers of the Great War.* (Penguin. 1978)

Winter, J. M. *The Great War and the British People.* (Macmillan Education Ltd. 1986)

Wootton, Graham *The Official History of the British Legion.*
(Macdonald and Evans Ltd. 1956)

The National Roll of the Great War 1914-1918; Section V; Luton.
(The National Publishing Co.)

Books about Luton

Austin, William *The History of Luton and its Hamlets,* V ols. I and II.
(The County Press. 1928)

Baker, Lionel *The Story of Luton and its Public Libraries.* (Luton Museum. 1983)

Bunker, S., Holgate, *The Changing Face of Luton.* R. & Nichols, M (Book Castle. 1993)

Cooper, Ken *Luton Scene Again.* (Phillimore. 1990)

Darby, Aubrey *Luton, Past and Present.* (Stalker. 1874)

Davis, Frederick *Luton, Past and Present.* (Stalker. 1874)

Dony, John G. *The 1919 Peace Riots in Luton.*
(Bedfordshire Historical Record Society, Volume 57)

Dony, John G. *The Story of Luton.*
(White Crescent & Dyer, James Press 3rd Edition. 1975)

Dyer, James *The Stopsley Book.* (Book Castle. 1998)

Hackett, Frank *Luton in Old Picture Postcards.* (European Library. 1982)

Hobbs, T. G.*Luton and Neighbourhood* Illustrated. (T. G. Hobbs. 1908)

Lea, Vic *Legacies. Tales and Legends of Luton and the North Chilterns.*
(Book Castle. 1993)

Madigan, T. J. *The Men Who Wore Straw Helmets. Policing Luton 1840-1974.*
(BookCastle. 1993)

Manning, W. H.*The Celebration of the Peace.* (University of Reading)

Smith, Stuart *Pubs and Pints. The Story of Luton's Public Houses and Breweries.*
(Book Castle. 1995)

Trevelyan, R. *Grand Dukes and Diamonds.*
The Wernhers of Luton Hoo. (Secker and Warburg. 1991)

White, Harold (Editor) *Luton Past and Present.* (White Crescent Press. 1977)

The Luton Year Book and Directory. (Various Editions)

Leaflets and Articles

Dony, John *How Luton Became a Borough.* (Bedfordshire Magazine)

Lea, V. W. *The Riot of Peace Day.* (Bedfordshire Magazine)

The 1919 Luton Peace Riot. Information Sheet No. 3. (Luton Museum)

The General Cemetery. (Luton Museum)

The Town Hall Clock. (Borough of Luton Architects Department. 1989)

Newspapers: *The Luton News*
                    The Luton Reporter
                    The Beds & Herts Tuesday Telegraph
                    The Beds & Herts Saturday Telegraph
                    The Bedfordshire Times
                    The Evening Post
                    The Daily Telegraph

Other Sources: *Luton Board of Health Minutes*
                    Luton Town Council Minutes
                    Luton Fire Brigade Reports
                    The DS&S Journals
                    The Peace Celebrations Programme
                    Correspondence from and to William
                    Smith, Town Clerk, Luton

Unpublished Sources

Bunker, Stephen *Strawopolis. The Transformation of Luton 1840-1876.* (University College, London. Ph.D. Thesis. 1991)

Dillon, Bernard *Frank Chapman Scargill 1836-1910.*

Freeman, Charles *The Luton Riots. A Reconstruction of the Events.* (Luton Library Ref. 942:565)

Lally, John *The Military Service Tribunal In Luton During the First World War.*
(University of Luton. 1998)

Mason, V. *The Riots of Peace Day.* (Luton Museum Ref. 91 77)

Turner, Christine *Luton Town Hall 1936.*

Where They Burnt The Town Hall Down

Luton, the First World War and
the Peace Day Riots of 1919